HOW TO MEET YOUR SELF

ALSO BY DR. NICOLE LePERA

HOW TO DO THE WORK

HOW TO MEET YOUR SELF

THE WORKBOOK FOR SELF-DISCOVERY

DR. NICOLE LePERA

HARPER WAVE

An Imprint of HarperCollinsPublishers

HOW TO MEET YOUR SELF. Copyright © 2022 by Nicole LePera. All rights reserved. Printed in the United States of America. No part of this book may be used or reproduced in any manner whatsoever without written permission except in the case of brief quotations embodied in critical articles and reviews. For information, address HarperCollins Publishers, 195 Broadway, New York, NY 10007.

HarperCollins books may be purchased for educational, business, or sales promotional use. For information, please email the Special Markets Department at SPsales@harpercollins.com.

FIRST EDITION

Designed by Leah Carlson-Stanisic

All art provided by Shutterstock, Inc.

Library of Congress Cataloging-in-Publication Data has been applied for.

ISBN 978-0-06-326771-8

22 23 24 25 26 LBC 6 5 4 3 2

This work is dedicated
to Jacob Weakland, whose divine
guidance helped channel the creation
of these pages, all of which were brought
forth in the weeks and months following
his physical passing.

Jake, you are so loved and your
presence is so felt.

CONTENTS

HOW TO MEET YOUR SELF

INTRODUCTION

Welcome to the beginning of a life-changing journey that has the potential to transform you at your very core. You've picked this book up for a reason. You may have sensed that something needs to shift in your life, and you're not alone in this feeling. If you're like most of us, you're probably stuck on autopilot, reliving the same habits day after day. You might know what you want to do differently but just can't seem to change, or you may feel unsure of where to even start. The reality is, most of who you are and what you do is determined by your past, not by your conscious choices today. This book is going to change that.

An empowering shift happens when we learn that we live most of our lives on autopilot and that we can awaken our consciousness to create new, healthy habits. By objectively and compassionately observing the physical, mental, and emotional patterns that fill our days and create our current selves, we can more clearly see what we do not want to carry into the future. Some people describe this shift as a sudden *awakening* or an *aha!* moment. For others, this realization comes slowly and makes more and more sense over time. That's what is so beautiful about this journey. It will happen in different ways and will mean different things to different people. It will be uniquely yours. For some readers, it may be the first time in years or decades you've put your focus and attention on yourself. That choice will have a profound impact on your life.

I've yet to meet a human who is fully aware of all the patterns that hold them back. We are all blind to parts of ourselves we are not yet willing, or ready, to face. Sometimes we are so focused on a particular *issue* that we don't even notice the different ways we ourselves play a role in perpetuating these difficulties. Only by understanding our habits are we able to change them to create space for a life of chosen purpose, compassion, and fulfillment. I created this workbook to serve as your guiding light, showing you a clear path to the truth of who you *actually* are.

In my first book, *How to Do the Work*, I shared my manifesto on how to understand and heal from the dysfunctional patterns that hold us back from living up to our fullest potential. I wrote about reparenting, trauma bonds, nervous system regulation, and the inner child. I received feedback from thousands of readers who all shared a hunger for more information. Many wanted to go deeper, to learn more about themselves, and to develop tools to help them continue to explore and grow. Many looked for guidance on how to actually *practice* self-observation, or self-witnessing, to help identify the different subconscious habits that were keeping them stuck. After all, we have to be conscious of our dysfunctional patterns before we can set out to change them. This workbook is the answer to those requests, with exercises throughout that provide a complete toolbox for fully witnessing and reconnecting with your authentic Self.

While doing the work and applying the practices in this workbook, you will begin to become aware of the different habits you may have been repeating since childhood. Our earliest childhood experiences are imprinted deep within us. As we grow older, it is these earliest experiences that we unconsciously re-create. If we didn't feel safe or have our needs consistently met by our caregivers as children, we can become stuck in painful cycles as adults. The journey you are about to take in this workbook will allow you to see yourself from a new perspective, unlocking layers of self-awareness that will open you up to a new way of living. The exercises throughout will help you fully witness yourself, without judgment, and release the patterns in your life that are holding you back or keeping you stuck.

I know all about feeling stuck. A few years ago I was a practicing therapist who felt exhausted, burned out, and unfulfilled. I was living in survival mode and my physical and emotional health was suffering. I'd wake up on Monday morning, drag myself out of bed and to work, and drift through the week mindlessly on autopilot. In the process, I consistently neglected my own needs as I worked tirelessly to try to *please* others, always worried about what they thought about or needed from me. Ironically, I was just as stuck and overwhelmed as the clients I was working with daily.

It wasn't until I had a health crisis (memory difficulties, terrible digestive issues, and fainting spells) that I was forced to *wake up* from life as I knew it. For the first time ever I prioritized myself, and started my own healing journey. As I showed up for myself and my own needs day after day, my life completely transformed. I felt a sense of purpose, I was taking care of my body, and I was finally processing all the trauma and wounding from my past that I had previously distracted myself from.

Soon, I started teaching others how they could do the same, and a global community of SelfHealers formed. Over the years, millions of people from around the world and from all walks of life have joined this empowering movement. Within every human are habits that trap us in cycles of misery, pain, and self-destruction. Within each of us is also the ability to show up every day, leaving behind those habits that no longer serve us and stepping into the highest versions of ourselves. Within each of us is the ability to trust ourselves enough to leave dysfunctional relationships and to find a safe and secure love. Within each of us is the ability to alchemize our trauma and begin to live a life of purpose. Within each of us is the ability to feel confident and empowered as we begin to consciously create a life on our own terms.

As your guide on this journey, I have to be fully transparent: this isn't going to be easy. You're going to see parts of yourself that have been hurt, betrayed, and abandoned. A lot of emotions may begin to bubble to the surface and some may wash over you all at once. If you're new to inner work, some of the concepts in this book might be things you've never thought about or talked about with friends or family. That's okay. At some point we are all new to this, and everyone goes through the feelings of doubt and fear, so you are not alone. In order to transform our lives, we have to get comfortable with gently pushing ourselves out of our comfort zone. Our comfort zone is what's familiar to us, and on this journey, you'll learn that what's familiar isn't always aligned with what is best for us. The more we show ourselves that it's safe to leave the familiar (*what we know*), the more we open ourselves up to the growth and expansion that are always available to us in any new moment.

I designed this book to be completely self-guided; it can be used at your own pace and all of the exercises can be completed wherever you feel most comfortable. If you need to take breaks, take them. There really is no *wrong* or *right* way to do this work. You're more than welcome to bring these exercises into therapy, share them with friends, or complete them with a partner who wants to begin their own journey. It's important to feel total agency to choose what is best for you—recovering our power to choose is foundational for each of us.

I believe a new paradigm is coming to mental health, one that assures us that there is nothing inherently *wrong* with any of us. The truth is you are resilient, capable, and possess limitless potential, and through this work, you're going to become an active participant in accessing those capabilities. In these pages, I've laid the foundation and you will become the builder of your future, even if it might be hard for you to envision right now. It's okay if you can't make out the details, all you need at this moment is the belief that you can change. Everything else will come with time and practice. Thousands of people from every walk of life have created profound transformation with the foundational tools that are presented in this book. And now, you can too.

Now, take a deep breath and let's begin.

HOW TO GET STARTED

BEGIN WITH THE INTENTION-SETTING EXERCISE ON PAGE 12.
This exercise sets the tone for this journey. It's important to take the time to complete it.

COMMIT THE TIME.
The amount of time you spend on this workbook will be different for everyone.
We all lead busy lives with many different obligations and priorities making it difficult
to set aside time just for ourselves. All you'll need is ten to fifteen minutes each day to
practice. These practices could become a ritual you create every morning when you wake up, or
something you do right before bed. You might even want to set reminders in your phone
or find a buddy to help hold you accountable for showing up.

GET CREATIVE.
You may want to grab some colorful pens or markers to do the exercises. You may even want to use a
separate notebook to do this work in, so you can make it your own. Whatever feels good, go with it.

CREATE A SAFE SPACE TO USE THIS WORKBOOK.
A safe space is somewhere you feel completely comfortable, at peace,
and open to new ideas. You can create this space in your bedroom, a certain nook in your
home, or even outside in nature. Ideally, you'll want this to be a space where you'll have full
privacy and won't be interrupted. You can add anything that makes you feel comfortable: maybe
light a candle or have a cozy blanket to wrap yourself in. Some of you may even listen
to relaxing music with headphones, or have your pet with you.
Spend some time to make this space completely your own.

BUILDING YOUR OWN INTERNAL SUPPORT SYSTEM

To build a foundation of support for our journey, we will want to identify the different ways we can help ourselves feel safe and secure along the way. None of us can control the world around us, so it's helpful to create a space within ourselves that allows us to respond to the world in healthy ways. I like to think of our internal support system as a toolbox we can access at any time, especially to help us get through difficult or stressful emotions.

Here Are Some Examples of Using Internal Support

- You find yourself feeling super anxious and can't really place your finger on why. You decide to go on a quick, brisk fifteen-minute walk around your neighborhood. You notice your emotions and thoughts shift and you're feeling a bit calmer when you get home.
- You woke up feeling sad and can't seem to find the motivation to do anything on your to-do list. You sit on your bed and decide that you're going to do a five-minute breathing technique. You notice you feel less upset and are able to do a quick chore that you've been putting off.
- After an intense conversation with your partner, you feel overwhelmed and notice some anger coming up. You do a simple grounding exercise, noticing the colors in the room and the way the ground supports your body. Afterward, you notice you broke up the cycle of intrusive thoughts and feel slightly less agitated. You then pick up your journal to express some of what you're feeling to help process the rest of your emotions.
- All day you've felt *off*. You notice that you've been criticizing and judging yourself throughout the day so as dusk comes, you commit to getting into bed early. Over time, you've noticed that you tend to feel this way when you need sleep and give yourself the rest you need to begin a new day tomorrow.

CREATING A SENSE OF SAFETY

Safety and security are integral to this healing journey of self-discovery. Using the tools below will help you build a foundation of inner safety you can access at any time. When we don't feel safe because of current circumstances, or because of trauma that continues to live in our body, we are not able to hear the pings from our authentic Self. Consistently accessing this safe space within will help you reconnect with this deepest part of you. Remember, it's not only okay to take breaks, it's important to do so. The more you practice, the more comfortable you'll become with the different uncomfortable sensations that may arise with this work.

Use Your Breath to Create Safety

Learning to use our breath is a powerful way to regulate our nervous system. When we experience stress, our breathing becomes shallow and quick. Sometimes, we might find ourselves holding our breath and clenching our jaw. These physiological shifts send our body a message that we are not safe, and that it's time to prepare for a threat. By learning how to intentionally change the way we breathe, we can teach our body that we are safe. Here are some of my favorite breathing exercises. You can try each of them, or just the ones you're specifically drawn to:

Balanced Breathing

- Sit or lay down in a comfortable position where you'll be able to safely relax for the next few minutes.
- Begin to inhale slowly and deeply through your nose to the count of five, relaxing your jaw, shoulders, and any other muscles that feel tense.
- Exhale slowly through your nose to the same count of five, feeling your body continue to relax.
- Repeat this pattern of inhalation and exhalation for one to two minutes.
- Check in with your body and notice any shifts or changes in its feelings of stress or tension.

Deep Belly Breathing

- Sit or lay down in a comfortable position where you'll be able to safely relax for the next few minutes.
- Place your hand(s) on your belly and begin to inhale slowly and deeply through your nose, feeling the air inflate your belly, relaxing your jaw, shoulders, and any other muscles that feel tense.
- Exhale slowly through your nose, feeling the air leave your body and your belly deflate.
- Repeat this pattern of deep belly breathing for one to two minutes.
- Check in with your body and notice any shifts or changes in its feelings of stress or tension.

Straw Breathing

- Sit or lay down in a comfortable position where you'll be able to safely relax for the next few minutes.
- Begin to inhale slowly and deeply through your nose, relaxing your jaw, shoulders, and any others muscles that feel tense.
- Exhale through pursed lips like you're slowly blowing air through an imaginary straw.
- Continue breathing slowly and deeply for one to two minutes, exhaling the air slowly through an imaginary straw.
- Check in with your body and notice any shifts or changes in its feelings of stress or tension.

4-7-8 Breathing

- Sit or lay down in a comfortable position where you'll be able to safely relax for the next few minutes
- Begin to inhale slowly and deeply through your nose for four seconds, hold your breath for seven seconds, and then exhale for eight seconds, relaxing your jaw, shoulders, and any other muscles that feel tense.
- Repeat this pattern of 4-7-8 breathing for one to two minutes.
- Check in with your body and notice any shifts or changes in its feelings of stress or tension.

Box Breathing

- Sit or lay down in a comfortable position where you'll be able to safely relax for the next few minutes.
- Begin to inhale slowly and deeply through your nose for four seconds, hold your breath for four seconds, and then exhale for four seconds. Wait four seconds before your next inhalation.
- Repeat this pattern of box breathing for one to two minutes.
- Check in with your body and notice any shifts or changes in its feelings of stress or tension.

Alternate-Nostril Breathing

- Sit or lay down in a comfortable position where you'll be able to safely relax for the next few minutes.
- Gently close your right nostril with your right thumb, and inhale slowly and deeply through the left nostril. Then close the left nostril with your right finger and release your thumb, exhaling slowly through the right nostril.
- With the right nostril open, inhale slowly and deeply, then close it with your right thumb, exhaling slowly through your left nostril.
- Once your exhalation is complete, inhale through the left and begin the cycle again, repeating this pattern of alternate-nostril breathing for one to two minutes.
- Check in with your body and notice any shifts or changes in its feelings of stress or tension.

Check In with Your Senses

In addition to regulating our breath, we can tap into our senses to feel safe in our body. Activating our senses helps us more fully focus our attention on the present moment, calming our body's stress response by helping us feel grounded, safe, and secure.

Take a moment to reconnect with your sensory environment by asking yourself the following questions:

What do I hear right now? What do I see? What do I taste? What do I feel touching my body or skin? What do I smell?

Experience

Using your senses helps to ground you, or to shift your attention away from your thinking mind to what's happening in your body or in your surroundings. This can be incredibly helpful when your thoughts are causing stress or emotional overwhelm.

Using the list below, pick one activity to practice this sensory grounding exercise. After spending a few moments reconnecting with your senses, check in with how your body feels.

Light a candle and spend a few moments simply watching its flame.

Burn some incense and spend a few moments smelling its aroma.

Grab a slice of an orange or other juicy fruit and spend a few moments as you slowly bite its flesh and taste its juices.

Find your pet or a favorite blanket and spend a few moments rubbing your hand over its softness.

Put on your favorite music and spend a few moments listening to the sounds and melodies.

Find Your Ground

Engaging with nature is a powerful way to calm a stressed body. When you spend a few moments reconnecting with the earth beneath you, the sights and sounds of the nature around you, or the sun above you, your stress hormones actually begin to decrease, helping you feel a bit safer.

Reconnect to the Earth

- Bring your attention to your feet and notice how the heel and sole of both feet make contact with the ground. Take your shoes off (*if possible*) for extra contact with the earth. Spend two to five minutes just feeling the ground underneath you.
- Surround yourself with nature by sitting in a garden or a local park, or visiting your plants and spend two to five minutes fully experiencing the nature around you.
- Stand in the sunshine and focus your attention on the feeling of its warmth on your skin.

Find Your Ground Guided Meditation

Nature Heals

Research consistently shows that being surrounded by nature for as little as twenty minutes can lower stress hormones. Even being in the sun for a few minutes can help increase serotonin and dopamine, chemicals that play a role in our feelings of well-being.

Find the nearest park, hiking trail, or even a spot in your backyard, or sit outside on the next sunny day and notice the effects of spending this time outdoors.

Visualize Safety and Relaxation

Take a seat, or lay down, in a comfortable space where you can safely relax and won't be interrupted. Close your eyes (if it feels safe to do so) and focus your attention on your breathing. Begin to picture a white, glowing light around your heart. As you continue to breathe deeply, imagine the white light becoming stronger and feel your heart softening and opening at the same time. As you begin to feel more relaxed, envision the white light filling the entire area of your chest and repeat aloud or silently to yourself: *"My heart is safe. I am safe. I am open and free."*

SET YOUR INTENTION

Now that you have a set of tools to help you find safety and security, it's a good idea to begin practicing these exercises as consistently as possible. Developing strong inner resources will help you continue to build the foundation of security needed for your journey toward your authentic Self.

For your pathway forward to appear, you must now get clear on where you are going. You do that by setting an intention. Before you set an intention, it's helpful to understand what an intention is. An intention is a purpose or goal that you've chosen to experience. It's an awareness of our state-of-consciousness and the forethought that allows us to become active participants in the way we show up in our life. In the following intention-setting exercise, the purpose or goal that you are choosing to pursue is the embodiment of your future and best self—your authentic Self.

To become your authentic Self, and live the life you want to live, you need to begin to explore *who* that person is and *what* that desired life looks like for *you*. You will want to spend time imagining what it *feels* like to *be* that person. The more detailed the vision and intention, the more powerful the result. Being intentional means taking consistent action, and the activities offered throughout this workbook will help you determine what that looks like for you.

Everyone's intention will be specific to them because we each have our own unique essence and purpose in the world. That's our work: to bring forth our authentic essence and purpose, and it's the follow-through of intention that allows this new Self to emerge.

You'll notice a core focus on ourselves along this journey. This is because we can only make changes to our own self, our own way of being, not anyone else's. While many of us may want to change or improve a relationship or to experience someone or some environment differently, that work begins with us. When we show up differently, so do the relationships and world around us. When we change ourselves, we change our world.

A few things to note:

- Though it is very common to do so, the following exercise is not a space to critique or judge your current self and environment. This is purely a space to close your eyes and imagine what it may look and feel like to actually *be* that highest version of yourself; to live their life, to be in their environment.

- It may be challenging to call to mind the details of what this desired version of you looks like and those details may change over time. That's okay! And it's perfectly normal. You can (and should) instead try to always focus on how it *feels* within your body when imagining this future you.

Let's begin:

1. Find a space where you can take a few moments to sit or lie safely and comfortably without interruption; close your eyes if you feel safe to do so.

2. Take a moment to envision the future you currently want for yourself, in as much detail as you can. Imagine what it's like to live this future life. Imagine what you're doing, where you are, how you feel, who you're with. Use the prompts on the following pages to help bring the details of this vision into your own mind. Practice focusing your attention on how your body feels as you begin to mentally and emotionally embody this future life.

3. Write down the details. There are no right or wrong responses here. We are simply imagining and letting our creativity flow. Remember to tune in to your body and how you feel physically while asking these questions. For example: you might want to practice embodying feelings of energy, lightheartedness, or ease in your body.

WHEN ENVISIONING YOUR FUTURE SELF . . .

How do you feel?

What are you doing?

What are you thinking?

Who are you spending time with?

Where and with whom are you living?

What are you most proud of?

What do you do for "work" or to financially support yourself?

How do you feel in your relationships (with romantic partners, friends, business associates, etc.)?

What self-care routines do you have?

How do you typically spend your day (mornings, afternoons, evening)?

**Set Your Intention
Guided Meditation**

Congratulations! You've just taken the first step toward meeting and becoming who you're meant to be, your authentic Self. The reason you can envision this version of yourself is because it's already within you. It's going to be a beautiful, enlightening journey to reconnect with this deepest part of you.

Now, let's continue the journey.

HOW WE MEET OUR SELVES

YOUR CONDITIONING:
YOU ARE NOT WHO YOU THINK YOU ARE

WHAT YOU'LL LEARN

What conditioning is and how it affects your life

How to identify your habit self

Why consciousness is the foundation of transformation

What neuroplasticity is and how to harness its power

When we are born, our brain is like a sponge. Wide-eyed, we take in everything around us. This is how we learn language, how to function within society, and how to interact with others and the world around us. It's remarkable just how much information we're constantly absorbing as we grow.

At birth, we are fully dependent on the most important people in our lives: our parent-figures. They're responsible for meeting all of our needs: feeding us, loving us, and keeping us safe. They make up our earliest environments and home. Within these relational environments are beliefs, ways of communicating, ways of expressing or coping with emotions, and other habits that we witness throughout our childhood. Our parent-figures (and the other close relationships we have) shape our world through modeling. We begin to embody the same thoughts, patterns, and behaviors that we saw in others around us. This is called our *conditioning*. As adults, many of us remain unaware that many of our current beliefs or habits may come from these early experiences and may not actually be the result of conscious choice.

Conditioning happens at the subconscious level. As babies and children, we don't consciously decide to store this information; our brain does it for us. Our subconscious mind (*subconscious* literally means below consciousness) stores the neural pathways that formed over time from the repetition of thoughts, behaviors, and other habits. It's not just our minds that store our conditioning, our body does, too. Our nervous system begins to form around six weeks in utero and continues to develop until the age of twenty-five. Our home environment and the relationships we experience within that environment actually influence the way our nervous system develops. If our first relationships were safe, secure, and predictable, our nervous system is typically *resilient* and able to recover from stressful experiences. If our first relationships were not safe, our nervous system becomes hypervigilant, always anticipating danger. Over time, a dysregulated nervous system can pave the way for dysfunctional coping mechanisms (substance use, reactivity, self-sabotage, excessive working), insecurity (or an inability to trust ourselves and others), and disconnection. When this happens, we don't feel safe in our own bodies, so we find ways to leave that threatening terrain.

The most common way people leave their bodies is through a process called *dissociation*, where our bodies are physically present but we are mentally gone somewhere else. People describe this experience as feeling haziness, confusion, or getting lost in thought or distracting behaviors, often losing large chunks of time. These days, many of us do this daily when we scroll endlessly on our phones, disconnecting from our body and wondering where our time goes. Dissociation was my learned way of coping, and is a reason that, as an adult, I actually have very few childhood memories. Escaping my body was a safe way to protect myself from experiences that felt too overwhelming for me as a child.

Like me, you may discover on this journey that you have beliefs, coping styles, and behaviors you continue to repeat even though they no longer serve you. None of us could choose the habits modeled to us in childhood, and it is unhelpful to think about them as *bad* or *good*—they are simply information we picked up in our earliest years, from adults who were doing the best they could with the level of awareness and tools they had modeled to them in the environments and circumstances in which they lived. Thankfully, now, as an adult, you have the profound ability to witness your conditioning and make space for new choices that are more in alignment with who you actually want to be (and who you actually are at your core).

MEET YOUR HABIT SELF

Our habit self is formed through our conditioning, or repeated past experiences. Our habits are biologically imprinted into our brain and our nervous system and include the different ways we take care of our physical body, navigate our emotions, express ourselves, relate to others, and behave in our communities and environments. All of these reactions are likely based on our childhood perception of what we needed to do or how we needed to *be* in order to feel approved of, safe, and loved. Because we were completely dependent on others to care for us, staying connected to those around us was necessary for our survival. This left us no choice but to adapt to the world around us. And so we did.

Some of us grew up with an overbearing parent-figure who monitored us closely—*how we dressed, what we thought, or how we acted.* Since being ourselves wasn't accepted or allowed in childhood, we may continue to be who we think *other* people want us to be or might develop a habit of looking to others to figure out how to behave. Some of us grew up in a home where a parent-figure yelled and frightened us when they were upset. In adulthood, we might develop a habit of micromanaging other people's feelings to avoid upsetting anyone or being on the receiving end of similar explosive behavior. Alternatively, we may hide parts of who we are, fearing we will be punished or shamed (*as we once were*) if we show them to others.

When we've had an emotionally distant parent-figure who didn't or couldn't connect with us to guide us through our difficult childhood emotions, we may develop a habit of keeping ourselves distant, disconnected, or distracted in our relationships. We don't do this because we want to hurt others, we do this because we are afraid of feeling rejected, abandoned, or ignored as we did in childhood. In order to cope, we continue to keep a distance from people because we don't want to experience that pain again. At the same time, we deeply crave emotional closeness, which causes us to be at conflict within ourselves.

As many of us know far too well, some of our habitual patterns can cause us harm. How often have you snapped at a partner or yelled at your child about a minor inconvenience, then quickly recoiled in shock at your reactivity? Or how often have you told yourself you're going to change something and within a few days you're back to the same behavior? Identifying with these examples means you're human. These patterns of reactivity and unhelpful habits are not who you are and are instead a product of what you experienced.

For most of us, our earliest habits and patterns were based primarily on satisfying other people's needs, not our own, so we continue to live our lives for other people well into adulthood. Chronic people-pleasing becomes a coping mechanism, and over time we end up feeling resentful and unfulfilled. At the same time, we may not even know what our needs are, so we remain understandably unable to meet them. For many of us, this cycle is almost entirely unconscious, occurring outside of our awareness.

To break this habit of sleepwalking through life, we are now going to learn how to become conscious so that we can see these patterns and "wake up" to a new way of living. When we are conscious, we are more aware of what we think, how we feel, and how we behave. Becoming conscious or aware in the present moment will allow us to make choices beyond our habit self to rediscover who we really are. We can learn to identify and understand our needs, creating space for us to practice new ways of meeting these needs rather than continuing to rely on the habits that are stored in our brains. Like many of you, I spent years living as a chameleon, doing things for external validation or because I felt obligated to put others before myself. Learning how to become conscious has allowed me to break those habits and learn how to connect to my intuitive voice within in order to meet my own needs.

CONSCIOUSNESS

Pause for a minute and close your eyes. As you close your eyes, pay attention to the thoughts that come up. Witness the sensations that arise in your body. Notice how your feet feel on the floor or how this workbook feels in your hands. Maybe you notice feelings of frustration or boredom. Maybe you immediately think of the chores you have to do. Congratulations, you've just experienced consciousness: the act of becoming aware of your thoughts, feelings, and bodily sensations.

At its simplest, consciousness is awareness of our internal and external experience. Many of us believe we are the voice within our mind, or our thoughts. We are so attached, or lost in those thoughts, that we are actually unconscious to the rest of our life experience. Hearing this, some of you may wonder *who you are* if you are not your thoughts. You are the thinker of the thoughts, the human being able to access conscious awareness to observe your own thoughts. You are not the thoughts themselves.

When we are not conscious, it's like we're sleepwalking through life in a state where things just happen to us. This state of reactivity is not only disempowering, it also results in many of us understandably feeling like victims of our circumstances. Living a conscious life allows us to experience life in the present moment. It allows us to actually begin to *choose* how we respond to our experiences and to the life around us. It's in the consciousness of the present moment that we find the ability to create and transform both ourselves and our world.

Of course, we won't always be conscious, and that's okay. It can be almost impossible to be conscious all of the time, especially at the beginning of this practice. The goal is to understand how to utilize consciousness to zoom out to a wider view of ourselves and our life experience. Below is a foundational practice called the Daily Consciousness Check-in. Within my global healing community, the SelfHealers Circle, each member begins with this practice, and the results are incredible. This is the pathway to awakening to the truth of who we actually are.

Create Consciousness Guided Meditation

Daily Consciousness Check-in

Now that we understand the *concept* of consciousness, we can begin to apply this practice in our lives using a tool called the Daily Consciousness Check-in.

Most of us spend the majority of our time in our heads, largely unaware of what's happening in or around us. In order to become truly aware of ourselves and our habits, we need to take a moment to disconnect from the stream of endless thoughts running through our minds all day, every day. Taking note of what you're paying most attention to will help you become more aware of yourself and your surroundings.

This exercise will help you become conscious of how often your subconscious autopilot, or your habit self, is calling the shots. When we're not conscious, our autopilot is making our choices for us. When you witness how much this is the case you can understand why you are not necessarily who you think you are; you are much more than the conditioned habits and patterns that have created your current reality and way of being. This awareness sets the foundation for becoming who you want to be (*and who you are at your core*).

To awaken consciousness and increase self-awareness, try practicing the following consciousness check-in. Set an intention to create three moments throughout your day when you can pause and check in with just two things: what you're doing and where your attention is at that moment. To help you remember and follow through, set an alarm or reminder on your phone for the morning, afternoon, and evening.

When your alarm goes off, notice and ask yourself the following:

- What am I doing?
- Where is my attention/what am I paying attention to? If I'm lost in thought, what am I thinking?

Using the space below, or the notebook that you've chosen, write down your answers to both questions each time your alarm goes off. Practice this from a space of self-compassion and curiosity, without judgment.

_____

_____

_____

_____

_____

_____

_____

_____

_____

_____

_____

_____

NOTICE YOURSELF

Are you fully immersed in what you're doing at the moment the alarm sounds? Whether it's washing dishes, watching TV, or talking with a loved one, are you fully engaged in the present moment?

Or, are you lost in thought about an argument you had earlier in the day, an overdue bill, a run-in with an ex, or an upcoming stressful situation at work?

Becoming aware of all our thoughts can be uncomfortable at first. You are not trying to change anything right now; you are simply gaining awareness of how conscious you are by observing where your attention is.

Morning check-in:

Afternoon check-in:

Nighttime check-in:

It's most helpful to continue practicing this consciousness check-in (i.e., *setting an alarm, noting your answers to the two questions about what you are doing and thinking*) until you become comfortable accessing moments of consciousness on your own throughout the day. Revisit this tool as often as needed. Remember, there is no set timeline for this work or for your journey overall. When I teach this practice within my community membership, I encourage people to spend at least thirty days consistently practicing this part of the work. Many members report that they return to this check-in when they feel like they need a refresher or find themselves slipping back into autopilot. Remember consciousness is the basis of all transformation, so this tool can and should be used throughout your life especially whenever you're called to practice it.

Consciousness-Building Exercises

As we now know, building consciousness means increasing our self-awareness. We only begin the process of becoming who we *want* to become by first cultivating nonjudgmental awareness of who we *are* right now. Choosing to redirect our attention fully to the present moment allows us that awareness. To get to where we are going, we must have an understanding of where we are starting.

There are many different ways that we can begin the practice of building consciousness each day. Remember, *consistency* is key here. We wouldn't go to the gym one day, lift a single weight, and expect to become stronger overnight. Consciousness and healing are much the same. It's the *consistent repetition* of the following practices/exercises that allows the new pathways in our brain to form (see page 33 for more detail on the science of rewiring our brain).

The five exercises below are practices you can use daily. Add them to your resource toolbox to access anytime. As you go through each exercise, take notice of your experience and write down your reflections.

Body Scan

Become aware of the physical sensations in different parts of your body.

- Find a place to lie or sit comfortably for the next few moments. If you feel safe to do so, you may choose to close your eyes.
- Take two deep, slow breaths, feeling your body begin to relax into this moment.
- Spend a few moments noticing the different sensations that may be present in all the different areas of your body.
- Starting at the top of your head, begin gently focusing your attention downward to your neck, shoulders, chest, abdomen, all the way downward to the tips of your toes.
- Use the space below to write down what you notice as you begin to pay more conscious attention to the different sensations present in your physical body:

_____

_____

_____

CONSCIOUS MOVEMENT

Become aware of how your body feels when moving throughout the day.

- Begin to consistently check in with your body's muscles, noticing changes in tension and flexibility throughout the day.
- Pay attention to what it is you are *doing* when you notice these changes.
- Practice being in your body when you're stretching, standing at the sink doing the dishes, walking to the mailbox, or working out. Notice the feeling of your muscles expanding and contracting as you engage in your daily activities. Notice when your shoulders are rested and relaxed or when they're tense and rigid. Notice when you're clenching your jaw, or holding or constricting your lungs or breath.
- Use this space below to write down what you notice as you begin to pay more conscious attention to your muscles and physical body:

_____

_____

_____

_____

_____

_____

_____

_____

_____

_____

_____

_____

_____

_____

SAVORING

Savoring allows us to find joy in the simplicity of life. Become aware of how often you take time to savor, or truly experience the fullness of, your moments. This includes savoring the food you eat, the music you're listening to, or the warm water of your shower.

- Begin to consistently check in with your five senses (*sight, sound, smell, touch, and taste*) to more fully experience the small moments throughout your day. Focus on your body's physical awareness and sensations.
- Practice when you are having a meal, drinking a beverage, listening to music, being in nature, or doing anything else that naturally activates your senses. Then begin to practice turning your attention more fully to savor your experience in that moment.
- Use this space below to write down what you notice as you begin to pay more conscious attention to the fullness of your daily experiences, noting how your experiences may change as you become more fully present to them:

_____

_____

_____

_____

_____

_____

_____

_____

_____

_____

_____

_____

_____

CONSCIOUS BREATHING

Become aware of how often you notice your breath.

- Begin to consistently check in and witness your breath throughout the day.
- Notice what experiences or thoughts shift your normal breathing pattern.
- Ask yourself the following questions: *Do you start holding your breath when thinking about or experiencing something stressful? When do you notice your breath getting quicker and shallower? When, if ever, are you able to breathe more slowly and deeply?*
- Use this space below to write down what you've noticed as you begin to pay more conscious attention to your breathing patterns:

_____

_____

_____

_____

_____

_____

_____

_____

_____

_____

_____

_____

_____

_____

CONSCIOUS LISTENING

Become aware of how often you actively listen to others when they are communicating with you. Active listening means you're hearing what a person is saying without thinking about how you'll respond or being distracted by something else entirely.

- Begin to consistently check in and witness your listening habits throughout the day.
- Begin to notice how often you get lost in your own thoughts when someone is speaking to you. *What is being talked about when this happens? What is your attention getting distracted by or what are you paying most attention to? When, if ever, are you able to truly listen to another without distraction?*
- Use the space below to write down what you notice as you begin to pay more conscious attention to your listening habits:

_____

_____

_____

HOW WELL DO YOU KNOW YOUR SELF?

As you prepare for your journey of self-discovery, it's helpful to have a benchmark for where you are beginning. Give yourself a few moments to take the quiz below. This quiz will help assess your current level of self-awareness and will be visited again (at the end of this workbook) to get a sense of how far you have come in discovering, uncovering, and embodying your true authentic Self. Remember to be compassionate with yourself, this is simply your starting point.

I know what activities I like to do for fun or what brings me joy.

____ I have no idea.

____ Kind of.

____ Absolutely.

I'm comfortable sitting in silence with myself and don't immediately need to distract myself or always be busy.

____ I have no idea.

____ Kind of.

____ Absolutely.

I know what is important or meaningful to me in my own life.

____ I have no idea.

____ Kind of.

____ Absolutely.

I know what inspires me or makes me feel uplifted.

____ I have no idea.

____ Kind of.

____ Absolutely.

I'm aware of what my different needs are.

____ I have no idea.

____ Kind of.

____ Absolutely.

I'm aware of how to ask someone to help me meet my needs (if I'm unable to meet them on my own).

____ I have no idea.

____ Kind of.

____ Absolutely.

When I'm overwhelmed, I'm able to ask for support.

____ I have no idea.

____ Kind of.

____ Absolutely.

I know when I don't feel safe in a situation.

_____ I have no idea.

_____ Kind of.

_____ Absolutely.

I know when I've reached a high level of stress or feel overwhelmed and shouldn't make any important decisions.

_____ I have no idea.

_____ Kind of.

_____ Absolutely.

I'm aware of what I am looking for in my relationships.

_____ I have no idea.

_____ Kind of.

_____ Absolutely.

I'm aware of why I did things in my past, and I understand myself at that time.

_____ I have no idea.

_____ Kind of.

_____ Absolutely.

I'm aware of when I'm not being kind to myself (e.g., self-shaming, criticizing, comparing).

_____ I have no idea.

_____ Kind of.

_____ Absolutely.

I know when my body needs to move and when it needs rest.

_____ I have no idea.

_____ Kind of.

_____ Absolutely.

I know the difference between when I'm actually hungry and when I'm eating to distract myself or numb my emotions.

____ I have no idea.

____ Kind of.

____ Absolutely.

When I'm upset, I'm aware of the pattern of behavior I usually engage in (e.g., silent treatment shutdown, yelling, distracting myself/dissociation).

____ I have no idea.

____ Kind of.

____ Absolutely.

I know when I'm people-pleasing or doing something because someone wants me to, rather than because I actually want to do it.

____ I have no idea.

____ Kind of.

____ Absolutely.

THE NEUROSCIENCE OF CHANGE

Though our habit self can keep us stuck in old patterns that may not reflect our true Self, the good news is that repeating the past doesn't have to be our destiny. The brain is not a static, inflexible organ but can change throughout the course of our lives, a quality known as *neuroplasticity*. In 1968, neuroscientist Bruce McEwen discovered that although stress changes the structure of the brain and can even cause shrinkage in certain areas, this impact was not always permanent. In fact, as he revealed, our brain has the ability to continually rewire itself by creating new neural connections, or synapses, over time. This finding proved for the first time that the adult brain was plastic or changeable, contrary to prior belief that it operated more like a computer with a set program.

Our brain is constantly rewiring itself by strengthening the frequently used synapses and neural networks, and pruning, or eliminating, the ones used less often. The thoughts and actions we repeat over and over each day make some synapses stronger, while other synapses weaken, leaving most adults with about half the neural connections they had in childhood.

Think about your own life. You've likely thought the same thoughts, recycled the same feelings, and continued the same behaviors countless times. By doing this, you've created pathways within your brain that have resulted in your present-day neurological structure. This neurological structure influences how you experience everything in your life. Thankfully, we have influence over our brain and its neural development, and we can engage in daily intentional practices to improve our brain's ability to grow new neural connections.

Keep These Three Things in Mind on Your Journey

1. New neural pathways are created through consistent, daily repetition.
2. Learning something new or trying something new is the best way to harness neuroplasticity. You've already done that by embarking on this journey!
3. As you create new neural pathways, there will be mental resistance, a natural discomfort we all feel around change. You might feel frustrated, want to procrastinate, or lack motivation to start or continue on. This is a natural part of the transformation process that we all face. The work is to just keep showing up.

Before we move on to the next exercise, it's helpful to understand the mental resistance you'll naturally experience along your journey. While our brain has the ability to change throughout life, there's a reason why changing our habits can feel so challenging and exhausting. Creating new neural pathways requires an immense amount of mental energy. Our brain is survival-driven and categorizes all unknown or unfamiliar experiences as possible threats on a subconscious level. Our brain has evolved to favor situations it can predict or have control over, driving the procrastination so many of us experience. Our survival-driven brain likes being able to predict our habitual outcomes. The unknown or uncertain feels threatening on a deep subconscious level, driving the fear and discomfort many of us experience around change. Entertaining thoughts of "just doing it later" or breaking new habits after only a short period of time is where most of us get stuck. Knowing that almost all of us have hit this wall of mental resistance can help alleviate the shame many of us feel for "failing" to make or sustain the changes we want for ourselves.

Because our habits (and the neural pathways they create) have been formed over years or decades of our lives, you should expect some degree of discomfort or anxiety on this transformational journey. The unknown is scary, so it's important to take breaks as you need to and be kind to yourself along the way. With practice and time, you learn you can confidently tolerate the uncomfortable.

A SMALL DAILY PROMISE TOWARD
Empowerment

Your subconscious mind doesn't actually want you to change—no matter how you reason with it, it prefers the perceived safety of your familiar habits. Through an endless stream of thoughts (*"I should be doing something else right now!" "Nothing's happening, why bother!"*) or new and uncomfortable physical sensations, our subconscious mind consistently resists change. Many of you have likely met this resistance when you've tried to create new habits, only to fall back into old patterns once the resistance became overwhelming. This is a normal part of change. Every time we return to our habits, however, we betray ourselves and erode our self-trust. Rebuilding this trust will be an empowering part of your transformation journey.

Create a habit of setting and keeping one small promise each day. Every time you keep this promise, no matter how small *(it's actually good to start small to keep resistance from overwhelming you!)*, you are showing alignment between your intentions and daily actions. This alignment will help you regain any lost trust, and noticing and acknowledging the small changes that begin to accumulate with these kept promises will empower you to stay the course.

AFFIRMATIONS

Affirmations are statements that can be said silently or aloud to help us create new synaptic connections in our brain. Because most of the affirmations you will be using represent the beginning of a new belief *(yes, beliefs are just practiced thoughts grounded in our lived experiences)*, you will likely feel awkward, uncomfortable, or maybe a little silly when you first start saying them. This practice might be especially challenging if you didn't hear many positive things about yourself as a child or if you didn't witness adults speaking positively about themselves. I designed these affirmations to be as approachable and grounded as possible, so they can benefit anyone at any point in their journey. If you commit to the practice of repeating these affirmations, they will begin to feel more possible and true over time. You will begin to notice that your brain starts to validate the affirmations by filtering evidence of their truth into your conscious awareness.

SELF-WITNESSING

Now that we understand what our habit self is, we're going to learn how to *witness* it. In order for you to get the most benefit from this workbook, *you'll need to meet yourself.* It's one thing to learn these concepts, but it's another thing to actually experience learning moments by actively participating in this powerful work.

It's time for you to meet *you.*

Self-witnessing is the act of observing ourselves. I imagine it as going outside of yourself to look from overhead, in other words, zooming out from your more narrow view of yourself and your experiences. Most of us spend our time focused on other people and their needs or experiences. We might worry about what our partner thinks of us, if our mom is going to approve of the decision we've made, or if a new friend is offended by something we said or didn't say. These reactions are likely based on our childhood experiences, when many of us had to focus on a parent-figure *(their emotions, their reactions, and their behaviors)* in order to feel safe. This state of being hyperaware of how others perceive us is called hypervigilance and is the beginning of our habit to externalize, or to only focus on the world outside of ourselves.

It's a pattern that runs deep with many of us, especially those who experience social anxiety and have an obsessive focus on being liked or accepted by others. Social anxiety is actually a symptom or message from our mind and body. Because so many of us have experienced hurt and pain in our past relationships, it makes sense that we could feel on edge, shaky, sick to our stomach, or unable to think in new social situations. What we experience as anxiety is the product of our mind and body saying, *"This is new, and I want us to be careful because in the past people have shown us that we aren't safe with them."*

When we are consistently focused only on others, we become disconnected from our own needs, both mental and physical. For example, when we're seeking a relationship partner, far too many of us become consumed with worry about whether we are liked by the other person. We rarely stop to ask ourselves if *we* actually like *them*, or explore how *we* feel in our body when we're around that person.

In order to reconnect with our authentic Self, we have to witness ourselves, meaning, we have to start to observe *our* thoughts, behaviors, reactions, and what our body is telling us. Self-witnessing may feel strange at first because many of us have never really seen ourselves. That's okay, just keep in mind that you can always take breaks if you notice yourself becoming overwhelmed. As you continue this practice over time, you'll become more aware of your needs, limits, and emotions.

If you've never practiced self-witnessing, you might not like what you see at first. You may find yourself consumed by self-judgment, criticism, and shame. It's important to practice objectivity, or neutrality, when witnessing yourself and resist the urge to assign meanings of *good* or *bad.* Many of us unconsciously assign a judgment to what we're thinking, experiencing, or doing. Begin to notice the words you use to assess different aspects of your reality as *good* or *bad* or how it *should* or *shouldn't be.* You might be surprised to find just how often you're at odds with reality, or how often you want things to be different. With time, you'll learn to relax into these moments, or surrender. Surrender is the act of allowing what is without attempting to change it.

As you begin your self-witnessing journey through the remainder of the exercises, remember it's okay to encounter certain things you don't like or struggle to accept. There are many times that I still struggle to accept parts of myself or things I experience; this is part of being human. Whatever you observe yourself noticing, thinking, or feeling is completely okay. There is a difference between incessant self-analysis, which is often critical, and self-witnessing. The goal of self-witnessing is to learn how to see ourselves clearly and in a way that is neutral, compassionate, and accepting. Keep this in mind as we continue onward to the next stop on our journey: witnessing our habit self.

How to Use
Affirmations

Repetition is key in creating new neural pathways, so you want to repeat these affirmations at least one time each day. This should take no more than one or two minutes.

You can write these statements down in a journal or put them on a sticky note inside your bedroom, on your refrigerator, or in your car—anyplace where you might see them throughout the day!

Breathe deeply and, as you speak, try to sense in your body what these affirmations would feel like if they were true. With practice, you'll get more comfortable doing this.

Affirmations for Self-Transformation

Every day I am learning more about who I actually am.

I am growing every day.

I am a powerful creator of my own life experience and I can choose how I respond to the world around me.

I am safe.

I am worthy of love and acceptance and I choose to give this to myself every day.

I appreciate myself and everything that makes me unique.

I have gifts within me that are slowly starting to reveal themselves.

My life has meaning and purpose.

I forgive myself.

My past does not define me.

I am proud of myself and all I've overcome to be who I am today.

Every day I am making choices that create a better me.

BE PRESENT TO *What Is*

We all have to do things we don't necessarily enjoy—washing dishes, taking out the garbage, returning phone calls or emails. Some of us make these undesirable tasks more difficult for ourselves when we create mental resistance to them. When we spend time in anticipation of the task, resisting the reality of the situation (by thinking about how much you *wish you didn't* or *shouldn't have to* do something), we end up creating more stress for ourselves.

Begin to practice empowering, or *owning*, your choice as a meaningful step toward your desired goal. Any time you notice your *have to* or *should* thoughts, practice changing them to *choose to* and reminding yourself why you are making that choice.

For example, "I *have to* (or *should*) do the dishes" could be changed to "I *choose to* do the dishes to provide myself a clean kitchen." Notice the different sensations you experience in your body as you verbalize this empowering shift in language.

HOW TO MEET AND TRANSFORM YOURSELF

As we are learning, most of who we are today is a product of our conditioning. As we learn to self-witness, we are going to have access to make new choices in our lives. The remainder of this workbook will provide a variety of exercises to help you continue your journey to meet your authentic Self. All of the exercises in the following sections will follow the transformation process outlined below:

STEP 1. SEE YOURSELF. Begin to witness/explore what circumstances, experiences, or people allow you to feel safe (*open and receptive*) and empowered to meet your needs.

- Become the objective observer to witness your conditioning (all of which you'll meet in sections two and three), which is determining most of your current choices.
- Become conscious and separate the patterns of your habit self from your authentic Self or your inner knowing (*intuition*).

STEP 2. EMPOWER YOUR SELF. Consciously choose to pay attention to the sensations associated with your intuition to help you meet the needs of your authentic Self (outlined in the following illustration) and to guide you through your changing daily experiences.*

AUTHENTIC NEEDS PYRAMID

You might be aware of the needs that must be met for human survival, like food, water, shelter, and oxygen. While the fulfillment of these needs allows us to stay alive, we all also have deeper needs that come from our soul or inner essence. Meeting our emotional and spiritual needs allow us to thrive, feel inspired, and be curious about and connected to the world around us.

This authentic needs pyramid will help you begin to understand and identify all of your needs. Exploring this pyramid will allow you to become more conscious of which needs are being met and which needs are not. As you begin to practice meeting your unmet needs throughout the remainder of this workbook, notice how you feel and how your life begins to shift.

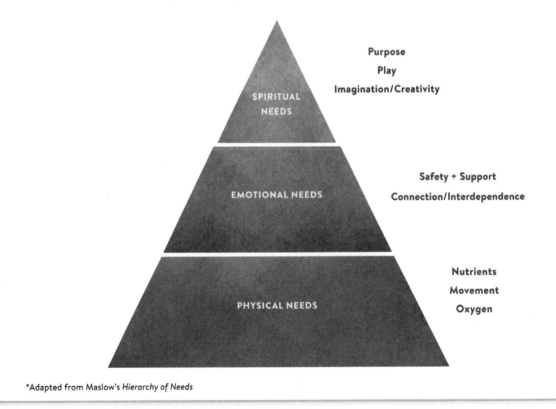

SPIRITUAL NEEDS

Purpose
Play
Imagination/Creativity

EMOTIONAL NEEDS

Safety + Support
Connection/Interdependence

PHYSICAL NEEDS

Nutrients
Movement
Oxygen

*Adapted from Maslow's *Hierarchy of Needs*

AFTER PRACTICING THE EXERCISES IN SECTION ONE YOU'LL KNOW HOW TO

Identify your habit self

Practice a consciousness check-in

Practice self-witnessing

Harness the power of neuroplasticity to create change

MEET YOUR HABIT SELF

RETURN TO YOUR BODY

WHAT YOU'LL LEARN

What it means to live in a conditioned body

What your current self-care habits are and how they impact you

What your body beliefs are and where they come from

How to practice body consciousness to begin to meet your physical needs

The next step in our journey is to return to our body. Many of us have left our bodies because we are overwhelmed, stressed, or have unresolved trauma making our physical self feel unsafe. We may have a complicated relationship with our body and be hyperfocused on appearance, or we may feel ashamed of our body, avoiding it at all costs. Whatever your current relationship may be, we are going to learn how to reconnect with and care for our body and its needs.

It is through taking care of our physical self that we are able to tolerate stress and other emotional experiences. If you've been disconnected from your body for a long time, many of your physical needs have probably gone unmet. As you learn how to identify and meet those needs, you will create a safe "home base" to return to after any upsetting experience.

When our physical needs are met, our body sends a message to our brain that we can relax within the present moment because we are safe. Similarly, our body is constantly sending messages to let us know when its needs are not being met. As you engage with the exercises in this part of the workbook, you will begin to witness your body sending you these signals. You may notice a grumbling stomach when you're hungry; sore muscles when you are tired, emotionally upset, or stressed; or quickened breathing when you are worried, anxious, or excited. This is all important information your body is offering you, and when you are connected to it, you can hear its messages and respond to its needs.

As you complete this section of the workbook, you're going to become more and more attuned to these subtle messages; this is a sign you're headed in the right direction. Of course, not all of us are privileged to live in a world that allows us to easily meet our needs. Many of us live in unsafe environments, don't have access to resources that support our well-being, have inflexible working hours, care for children or elders, or contend with other priorities that require much of our attention. Regardless of our circumstances, the more we can listen to our bodies, the more we can begin to take any small actions available to us to help better meet its needs.

WHERE SELF-CARE HABITS
COME FROM

Self-care is a buzzword in today's culture for a reason: the way we care for ourselves impacts every aspect of our lives, including our relationships with other people. The term is often used in reference to a luxury, like getting a facial, taking a vacation, or pampering ourselves in some way. While these activities can be examples of self-care, the self-care we are going to focus on here is simpler and more essential. Together, we'll explore the small ways we can take care of our physical body, our emotional states, and ultimately our spiritual needs. This can look like drinking a glass of water when we're thirsty, cooking a nourishing meal when we're hungry, asking our partners or community for help when we feel overwhelmed, or choosing to place a boundary when we need to rest or recharge.

When we were children, our parents and other adults often cared for us in different ways over time because our physical and emotional needs changed as we grew. If, overall, our parents cared for us with love, compassion, acceptance, and patience, we likely internalized the belief that we are *worthy* of being cared for and having our needs met. Over time, we usually end up learning how to take care of ourselves.

If, by contrast, our parents cared for us with hostility, resentment, anger, apathy, or an overall lack of patience, we may internalize the belief that we are a burden, unworthy of care or having our needs met. We carry these beliefs with us over the years and usually end up learning how to abandon or neglect ourselves and our own self-care.

In my work, I've found there are five styles of self-care that are typically modeled within families. On the opposite page, I've listed these styles and offered examples for each. Take some time to read through and note any that resonate with your childhood experiences.

NEGLECTFUL OR ABSENT

____ Physical needs largely unmet (as is common in homes where parents held multiple jobs, were dissociated or distracted, or engaged in addictive behaviors)

____ Little awareness or prioritization of eating nutritious meals, movement/rest, sleep hygiene, consistency, or boundaries, often resulting in physical self-neglect

EMOTIONALLY WITHDRAWN OR OVERWHELMED

____ Physical and material needs consistently met, though emotional needs mostly ignored

____ Emphasis is on appearance, achievement, or survival, often resulting in approval-seeking behaviors

OVER-INVOLVED OR HELICOPTER PARENTING

____ Hypervigilance around physical needs and/or appearance

____ Fear-based overinvolvement or control, often resulting in reliance on external guidance or validation

CRISIS CARE

____ Physical needs met most consistently (and sometimes only) in times of health crisis

____ Closeness and connection felt through sickness or crisis (as is common in homes with chronic health issues or addictive behaviors), often resulting in emotional need entanglement (or confusing another's needs for our own) or attempts to get emotional needs met through acts of physical care

VIOLATING OR ABUSIVE

____ Physical need for safety actively violated or weaponized (as is common in households where active physical, verbal, or sexual abuse is present)

____ Emphasis on survival *only* with overall neglect of other needs (emotional or *spiritual*)

Once you've gained awareness of the style of self-care you experienced in childhood— and have reflected on how your parent-figures cared for themselves—you can begin to better understand your current self-care habits and establish new, more supportive ways of caring for yourself.

Just as our minds have been conditioned, so have our bodies. Our body typically operates on autopilot: eating, moving/resting, and sleeping based on a routine we usually don't even have to think about. Thankfully, unconscious processes take care of our digestion, breathing, metabolism, hormonal balance, and the various other processes that keep us alive.

Starting in childhood, we witness and begin to repeat self-care habits that eventually get stored within both our minds and bodies. In addition to how our body is actually cared for, we are always watching how our parent-figures eat, speak about, and take care of *their* bodies. Those of us who had a parent-figure who was critical of their body might feel shame or low self-confidence around our body. Others who had a parent who was always dieting or depriving themselves of food may adopt these same habits, believing that losing weight will make them *"good enough"* or *"worthy"* of love and acceptance. These messages can be further reinforced through media messaging that has historically depicted thin bodies as more beautiful or desirable than other bodies.

Sometimes the messages we received about our bodies were far more direct. Many of our parents consistently commented on our physical appearance, restricted our diets, or compared our bodies to those of siblings, cousins, classmates, or friends. The message we receive as children led us to form the beliefs that: *"My body isn't good enough," "My body isn't lovable,"* or *"Other bodies are more worthy of love and acceptance," "I need to look like them so that my body can also be worthy of love and acceptance."*

Aside from comments on the physical size of bodies, it's also important to acknowledge other types of body shaming. Growing up, many of us rarely saw diversity in skin color, ethnicity presented in television, media, and movies. This lack of representation has a deep impact, sending us the subconscious message that there is a specific version of who is acceptable, attractive, or desirable in our society. Thankfully, we are beginning to see a shift in these practices, with a greater representation of diverse bodies in mainstream media. This is an incredibly important step in helping marginalized people access a deeper level of body acceptance, though there is still much work to be done.

Contrary to the messaging we receive from media, entertainment, and within our families, our body isn't what makes us lovable or unlovable. There is actually no such thing as a universal version of attractiveness for all humans. We are unique beings with a wide variety of body types, all of which are beautiful and worthy, regardless of what messages we have internalized.

This conditioning, or messages we internalized, are called body beliefs. Most of our body beliefs are subconscious (meaning we aren't even aware we have them), yet they impact our relationship with our body, our behaviors, and our self-worth. In this next section, you're going to identify your body beliefs so that you can begin the process of unlearning those that are unhelpful or inaccurate and develop a more loving relationship to your unique physical form.

YOUR INHERITED BODY BELIEFS

How did your parent-figures (or other caregivers) care for their own bodies?

How did your parent-figures (or other caregivers) talk about their own bodies?

How did your parent-figures (or other caregivers) talk about your body?

When you were young, do you have a memory of admiring a person's beauty or a specific body type? If so, what did this person look like?

How did your parent-figures (or other caregivers) speak or talk about weight or people's appearances?

If conversations about diet, weight loss, or weight issues were common in your home growing up, what was said or communicated?

I want to pause and acknowledge that uncovering body beliefs can bring up a lot of emotional pain or conflicted feelings. You may have heard the people you love speak about their own bodies or your body in a negative or hurtful way. You may need to take a break or allow yourself some space to process these emotions. In order to create a healthier relationship with our body, we have to release some old emotions we have carried, and I want to applaud you for having the courage to do this. I know firsthand that it's not easy, and as someone who's learning a better relationship with my body, I will remind you it's a lifelong journey.

Now that we have identified some of our inherited beliefs, we can move on to exploring how we think about and *feel in our body*.

HOW DO YOU FEEL IN YOUR BODY?

Body image is the mental picture you have of your body that is impacted by the body beliefs you inherited. The way you *think* and *feel* about your body shapes how you *see* yourself when you look in a mirror or at a picture and how you imagine others see you.

Healthy body image is about accepting your unique body, whatever its shape or size, and being comfortable in your own skin. It allows you to live presently in your body as opposed to constantly worrying about what others are thinking or how they are experiencing your physical self. There has been a recent movement toward *body positivity*, or embracing and loving your body as it is, which is a beautiful thing. I also want to suggest that it's completely okay if you don't love every part (or any part) of your body. Your feelings are going to change, grow, and shift as you continue through this process. The practice is to be okay with *however you feel*. Take some time now to begin to explore:

What do you currently think about your body?

How do you currently feel about your body?

What do you imagine others think and feel about your body?

What part(s) of your body do you love or appreciate?

How often and under what circumstances (or when) are you tempted to compare your body to others?

How often and under what circumstances (or when) do you find yourself commenting on other people's bodies (e.g., those of friends, strangers, people in TV/movies)? What is it that you're usually commenting on?

When you look at yourself getting dressed or in the mirror, what kind of thoughts do you have?

How often and under what circumstances (or when) do you scrutinize your appearance or make self-deprecating comments like "I look terrible," "I look like a mess," or "Ignore how terrible I look"? What do you say to or about yourself?

How often and under what circumstances (or when) do you buy clothes or try to hide parts of your body? What parts of your body do you try to hide?

How often and under what circumstances (or when) do you avoid situations where part of your body might be exposed and seen by others (for example, canceling plans that involve wearing a swimsuit), or avoid situations where you and your body are seen in general?

How often and under what circumstances (or when) do you change your appearance or clothing choices based on feedback from others or the media?

How often and under what circumstances (or when) do you refuse to buy certain clothes for your body (for example, only allowing yourself to buy clothes when you're the "right size")?

How often and under what circumstances (or when) are you comfortable with your partner(s) (or people you're sexually intimate with) seeing your body?

How often and under what circumstances (or when) do you use food or weight as a way to punish or reward yourself (for example, not buying clothes if you aren't the "right size," restricting food, self-shaming if your weight fluctuates, etc.)?

How often and under what circumstances (or when) do you use starvation techniques, pills, or extreme dieting in order to have a certain type of body?

YOUR BODY LANGUAGE SPEAKS

After gaining an awareness of what you *think* and *feel* about your body, let's begin to explore how your body itself may be both reflecting and impacting your self-image. Self-image is reflected in your posture and how you carry your body, your ability to take up space, and the way you move through life. These nonverbal signals sometimes communicate more to others and your surroundings than your words!

When you feel secure or safe, you are able to relax into your body as well as the space around your body. You are able to be physically seen by others and are open and receptive to eye contact. When you feel insecure or unsafe, your body language will reflect that lack of safety and send signals of fear or threat to those around you. You may feel uncomfortable being physically seen by others and may avoid maintained eye contact.

Spend the next few days (or weeks) witnessing your body language—including your posture, facial expressions, and eye contact—in all of your environments and relationships (e.g., at work, standing in line or riding public transportation with strangers, sitting at home alone or with a close loved one) to notice any variations in the following:

How often and under what circumstances (or when) do you feel comfortable being physically seen or contacted by others?

How often and under what circumstances (or when) do you hide yourself physically from others or avoid physical contact?

What does your overall body posture look like? Do you sit or stand with your arms or legs crossed, appearing closed off from the world around you? Do you sit or stand with your arms or legs comfortably open, appearing receptive to the world around you?

How often and under what circumstances (or when) do you notice yourself trying to make your body appear smaller or take up less space by blending into the background or hunching your shoulders?

How often and under what circumstances (or when) do you find yourself apologizing for certain aspects of your physical being or your overall physical presence?

How often and under what circumstances (or when) are you able to hold eye contact with others? How often and under what circumstances do you find eye contact difficult?

Body Language

Now that you are becoming aware of the messages your body language may be sending you and others around you, you can begin to practice changing these messages by changing the way you live in and carry your body.

STEP 1. Take a look at the differences between body language that is secure, safe, open, and receptive, and that which is insecure, unsafe, closed, and shut-down. Spend the next few days (or weeks) witnessing your body language and noticing what messages your body may be communicating to others and the world around you.

STEP 2. Practice embodying the different aspects of secure body language and notice any changes in the way you feel in your body.

INSECURE (CLOSED AND SHUT-DOWN)	SECURE (OPEN AND RECEPTIVE)
Rounded or hunched shoulders	Tall and straight shoulders
Tense and fearful facial muscles	Relaxed and softened facial muscles
Arms folded in front of body	Arms relaxed, hanging alongside body
Fidgety	Firmly grounded

MEET YOUR PHYSICAL HABIT SELF

Before we can begin creating new, lasting self-care habits that serve our authentic Self, we have to become aware of our *current* habits. In the following exercises you are going to do just that: meet your habit self.

As you do the work in the following exercises, it's helpful to remember that our goal is to simply *witness* and observe our current reality. There is nothing to fix or change here. This is going to be difficult for many of us because we spend an incredible amount of energy trying to fix or change ourselves. Establishing new habits is never easy, and the new habits you're developing here aren't any different.

As you begin observing your awareness and understanding of your needs and daily habits, remember to be honest, loving, and compassionate with yourself. The awareness you are cultivating is what will allow you to better meet your authentic needs and create habits that support and align with your highest Self. Let's begin.

Spend the next few days (or weeks) beginning to witness your daily habits. You might find it helpful to set daily reminders, such as an alarm on your phone, to remember to consciously check in and observe your patterns throughout the day. Chances are, you'll see the same daily habits repeated over and over again throughout your week. Begin to take notice of patterns. Write down your findings and reflections in the space below or in your chosen notebook.

WHEN YOU FIRST WAKE UP: Witness and note the first things you do after you wake up. This may take practice. Observe your first thoughts, feelings, and actions if you're able to identify them:

_____

_____

MORNING ROUTINE: You might be surprised to know everyone has a morning routine; most of us just aren't conscious of what that routine is. Witness and note the typical steps you take to get yourself ready for the day. These habits may include washing, eating, dressing, and any other activities you would consider part of your transition from sleeping to the day:

_____

_____

EATING ROUTINE: Witness and note the typical steps you take to obtain and consume your meals:

- When do you eat (e.g., at a certain time of day, when others are eating)?
- What do you eat and how do you decide? Do you have rules about what you *can* (or *can't*) or *should* (or *shouldn't*) eat (e.g., are there certain foods that are appropriate to eat only at certain times, like sweets or desserts only after a meal)? Note: these rules are different from religious or culturally based requirements.
- How are meals made (e.g., do you cook at home, eat out)?
- Where do you eat (e.g., do you always sit at a table, eat while on the go or commuting)?
- Do you have a particular approach to eating (e.g., do you always save one bite, do you eat everything on your plate)?

_____

_____

LEISURE TIME ROUTINE: Witness and note how you spend time when you're not working or fulfilling responsibilities in your life:

- Do you have leisure time? If not, why?
- If you do have leisure time, how do you typically spend it?
- How did you decide to spend your time that way?

_____

_____

NIGHTTIME ROUTINE: Observe and note the typical steps you take to wind down and get yourself ready for sleep at night (e.g., taking a bath, reading, watching TV, using your phone):

_____

_____

WELLNESS CHECK-IN

N ow that you are becoming conscious of your habit self, it will be helpful to begin exploring whether your daily routines are actually meeting your physical needs.

The following checklist will help you to become aware of your current self-care habits. Be honest and objective with yourself here. Remember, to get to where we want to be, we must first have an accurate awareness of where we are right now. Consider the prompts below and mark the response(s) that resonate most:

DO I FEED MY BODY THE NUTRIENTS IT NEEDS?

_____ I listen to my body, eating when it's hungry and stopping when full.

_____ I eat foods that help me feel full and energized when available.

_____ I am aware of foods that make me feel lethargic or jumpy (or otherwise unwell) and avoid them when possible.

_____ I typically feel mentally alert and sharp.

DO I MOVE MY BODY?

_____ I find ways to move my body a bit each day.

_____ I know when my body needs to rest or take a break.

_____ I feel connected to my body's energetic needs overall.

_____ I notice shifts in how I feel when I move my body.

DO I GIVE MY BODY ENOUGH REST?

_____ I fall asleep quickly after getting into bed.

_____ I am able to sleep through the night without waking (or when I do wake, I can fall back asleep).

_____ I wake up feeling refreshed and rejuvenated.

_____ I notice how lack of sleep affects my moods and behavior.

CAN I DEAL WITH STRESS?

_____ I am aware of how the people in my life affect my stress level.

_____ I am aware of how the content I consume (social media, news, entertainment) affects my stress level.

_____ I know when I'm stressed out and find moments to calm myself whenever possible.

_____ I find stillness, quiet, or nature for at least a few moments each day.

Many of you completing this checklist may discover that you are currently disconnected from your physical needs, likely because you are disconnected from your body. We are now going to start the journey of reconnecting to the body.

BODY CONSCIOUSNESS
Trauma Body

Before we talk about creating body consciousness, it's important to understand why so many of us are disconnected from our physical selves. For a long time it was believed that trauma was primarily a psychological phenomenon. Research on post-traumatic stress disorder (PTSD) focused mainly on the mental symptoms of trauma, including flashbacks, nightmares, or intrusive thoughts after a traumatic event. Under the framework of PTSD, trauma is understood as the result of enduring terrifying and life-threatening experiences such as war, severe abuse, or sexual assault.

The new research of polyvagal theory, founded by the neuroscientist and psychiatrist Dr. Stephen Porges, illustrates how trauma affects our bodies right alongside our minds. Under this framework, trauma itself is no longer defined solely by the type of *event* we experience but instead as the impact (specifically to our nervous systems) that results from being overwhelmed and under-supported in the face of all types of overwhelming experiences.

Our ability to tolerate stress and other challenges depends on the function of our nervous system and in particular, the function of a nerve called the vagus nerve. Our vagus nerve runs from our brain to all of our organs, facilitating communication between all parts of our body. After a stressful event has passed, a healthy, functioning vagus nerve tells the nervous system that it's safe to relax. But when we don't have safe and secure relationships to help us process difficult events, the vagus nerve may never send that message, and our nervous system activation persists, resulting in chronic dysregulation.

Those of us who had the benefit of consistent emotional support after overwhelming events are often less impacted by them than those of us who were left emotionally alone. Truly understanding and utilizing the impact of social support will, I believe, inspire community healing environments (both in real and virtual life) to become more prominent in the mental health field.

We are most vulnerable to the lasting effects of trauma as children, both because our nervous system is still developing and because when we are young, it is easy for us to feel threatened or unsafe. When we experience an event that overwhelms our ability to cope, the autonomic nervous system (ANS) steps in to help us survive the perceived threat. Notice I said *perceived* threat, something that is dictated by our age, environment, and our level of emotional development. The autonomic nervous system is a part of our central nervous system that ensures our survival by regulating the body outside of our conscious awareness. It responds to threats in three ways: fight or flight, freeze, or fawn (we will discuss these stress responses in more detail later). Ideally, after the threat has passed, our body begins its recovery process, allowing us to return to a feeling of safety, peace, and calm.

Chronic stress, dysfunctional environments, and a lack of predictability or safety can create an environment in which our autonomic nervous system gets stuck cycling through a stress response. This happens when our vagus nerve is not functioning properly. Unable to leave a state of dysregulation, we can remain stuck in these activated cycles for years or even decades of our lives. The state of our nervous system has a profound impact on how we relate to ourselves, how we relate to others, and how we interact with the world around us. When we live in an extended period of nervous system activation, we can enter what is called the trauma body, or a chronic state of survival mode. I believe that a large majority of the population exists within this survival mode, leading to sky-high levels of depression, anxiety, addiction, and other mental health issues.

The effects of chronic nervous system dysregulation are varied and can include:

- Dissociation, or a distracted, spacey, or numb feeling, and derealization, or confusion over what is actually happening or what's *real*;
- Hypervigilance/Hyperarousal, or chronically scanning the environment for danger (often presents as social anxiety);
- Fawning, or people-pleasing by ignoring one's own needs in order to avoid conflict or tension by serving or meeting the needs of others;
- Hypovigilance/Hypoarousal, or avoidance, isolation, or depression-like states.

In each of these reactions, our body is sending us a clear message: *I do not feel safe.*

Existing long term within a trauma body can lead to exhaustion, insomnia, high emotional reactivity, feelings or thoughts of doom or dread, and the inability to connect with others. Some people have described this experience as having a life run by fear-based decisions, often feeling completely out of control. In this state, we lose access to our intuition, creativity, and our ability to emotionally connect with others.

Your Nervous System's Stress Response

Spend some time with the chart on the opposite page, which offers a detailed explanation of the various states of the polyvagal response within the body. As you read through, consider what response(s) you notice most frequently in your body. Some of you may have blended responses, meaning your nervous system may respond in multiple ways at once. You may also notice that different situations you encounter activate different states.

Neuroception

Your nervous system is constantly assessing your environment and sending information to your brain through an unconscious process called neuroception. This felt data helps your brain determine whether your environment is safe or dangerous. The nervous system scans both your external environment (e.g., the look on your partner's face, the noise behind you) and your internal environment (e.g., the increase in your heart rate, the trembling in your muscles). If the brain detects a threat, it will initiate a stress response (fight/flight/freeze/fawn) via the nervous system. Once activated, this response continues to signal your body's state of stress to your brain until the perceived threat has ended. In simple terms, through the process of neuroception, a stressed-out body will unconsciously continue to scan its environment for stress until its state of activation changes.

Using the checklist on page 63, identify whether your body's dysregulated nervous system is keeping your neuroception on high alert.

SAFE AND SOCIAL RESPONSE (PARASYMPATHETIC, VENTRAL VAGAL*)	FIGHT-OR-FLIGHT RESPONSE (SYMPATHETIC)	FREEZE OR DISSOCIATE RESPONSE (PARASYMPATHETIC, DORSAL VAGAL*)	FAWN RESPONSE (BLENDED SYMPATHETIC AND PARASYMPATHETIC)
You feel safe to authentically connect with others and the world around you (authentic Self).	You feel unsafe and attempt to protect yourself through action (mobilization).	You feel unsafe and attempt to protect yourself by shutting down (immobilization).	You feel unsafe and attempt to protect yourself by being hypervigilant to others/your external environment.
Your body's internal systems are healthy and balanced (this is called homeostasis). Your digestion and sleep are uninterrupted and you feel energetic and able to think clearly.	Your body's internal systems are dysregulated. Your digestion is disturbed, your sleep is interrupted (e.g., difficulties falling or staying asleep), and you are not able to think clearly.	Your body's internal systems are dysregulated. Your digestion is slowed, your sleep is interrupted (e.g., oversleeping, difficulties waking), you are not able to think clearly or at all, and you feel numb or lethargic.	Your body's internal systems are dysregulated. Your digestion is disturbed, your sleep is interrupted (e.g., difficulties falling or staying asleep), and you are hyperfocused on the external world (e.g., others, your environment).
You feel safe being in your own body and are able to compassionately connect with others, the world around you, and something greater (e.g., the natural world or universe).	You don't feel safe and have feelings of alarm, anxiety, or hypervigilance/hyperarousal (constantly scanning for threat).	You don't feel safe and have feelings of fogginess, numbness, or hypoarousal (like you are going through the motions without awareness).	You don't feel safe and are hypervigilant or obsessively focused on your external environment.
You are able to regulate through stress and other emotional experiences (this is called self-regulation). You are able to stay connected with others through stress and other emotional experiences (this is called co-regulation).	You have difficulty thinking clearly or creating new solutions to current issues and usually attempt to find safety by acting aggressively (fighting, throwing a tantrum), or escaping the situation (fleeing, distracting).	You have difficulty thinking clearly or creating new solutions to current issues and usually attempt to find safety by disappearing, shutting down, or disconnecting.	You have difficulty thinking clearly or creating new solutions to current issues and usually attempt to find safety by fawning or people-pleasing to avoid the threat all together.
You feel safe enough to engage with others socially, are able to communicate attentively and effectively, and can both extend and receive support.	You feel out of sync with or disconnected from others and tend to misread social cues (usually perceiving threats where none are present), to be judgmental or critical of others, or to act selfishly.	You feel disconnected from others and the world around you, often feeling lost, abandoned, powerless, hopeless, or invisible.	You feel unseen, unacknowledged, taken advantage of, and often overly responsible for and resentful of others.

*Polyvagal theory founded by Dr. Stephen Porges.

IS YOUR BODY'S NERVOUS SYSTEM DYSREGULATED?

Take a look at the checklists beginning on the opposite page and spend the next few days (or weeks) witnessing your body to identify whether your nervous system is regulated or dysregulated. If you find that dysregulation is your baseline, don't worry. You can begin to heal this physical aftereffect of trauma by committing to the practices on pages 68–74, which teach your body how to feel safe in the present moment. The checklists will just give you an awareness of your starting point.

Note: If you never feel safe, or live in an environment in which there are active threats to your physical well-being, I encourage you to seek help and support immediately.

SIGNS OF A REGULATED NERVOUS SYSTEM

BODY

____ I am safe and connected to my physical body.

____ I feel relaxed and alert.

____ My heart rate is slow and regular.

____ I am connected to my emotions or the different sensations that run through my body.

____ I am able to cope with stress or emotional upset and bring my body back to feeling safe (or peaceful and calm) fairly quickly.

MIND

____ I am open to others and the world around me.

____ I am curious and able to be creative.

____ I am available and receptive for connection with others.

____ I am able to think clearly and plan for the future.

____ I am able to respond (instead of reacting) when I'm stressed or emotionally upset.

BREATH

____ My breath is slow and even.

____ My breath is even and from deep in my belly (it is not constricted, faint, or shallow in my chest).

SIGNS OF DYSREGULATED NERVOUS SYSTEM

BODY

____ I feel unsafe in my physical body and may feel anxious or panicked.

____ My heart rate is elevated.

____ My body is sweating or shaking and I feel uncomfortable in my own skin.

____ I am hyperaware of or numb to my emotions or bodily sensations.

____ I am unable to feel relaxed or comfortable and feel unsettled.

____ My body feels exhausted or depleted.

____ I feel tension throughout my body (in my neck and shoulder, jaw, or lower back, for example) or experience chronic pain (or other intense sensations) that moves to different places in the body.

MIND

____ I have racing thoughts or thoughts of hopelessness, despair, or criticism.

____ I have difficulty concentrating on tasks or thinking clearly and critically.

____ I feel "spaced-out" or unsure of what is real or what is imaginary.

____ I find myself seeking chronic distraction (watching TV, daydreaming, using substances).

BREATH

____ My breath is barely noticeable or constricted (I may even be holding it).

____ My breath is fast and shallow, coming from my chest (instead of my belly).

COPING WITH A DYSREGULATED NERVOUS SYSTEM

B y now many of you may be noticing the ways you are not truly living *in* your body. You may witness yourself living most of your life in your head, or your *thinking* mind. A mind full of constant chatter.

Many of us learned to distance ourselves from the discomfort of a dysregulated body by distracting ourselves with our thoughts. While these coping habits developed as our best attempts at regulating our nervous system and creating a sense of safety, they continue to keep us disconnected from our body and the inherent wisdom within us.

Take a look at the illustration below and the questions on the following pages to begin exploring the coping habits you've developed in response to a dysregulated nervous system. Spend the next few days (or weeks) witnessing your body's different nervous system states using the exploratory questions that follow.

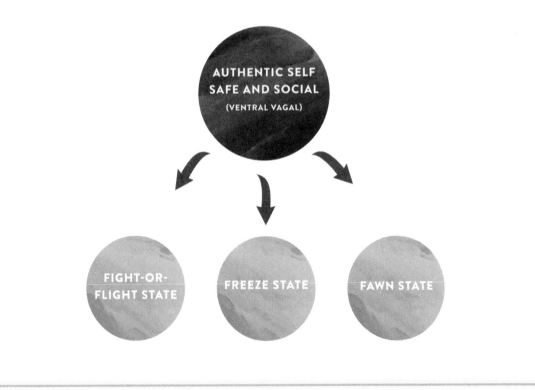

Fight-or-Flight State

- Habit of distracting/distancing from your physical body to find safety
- Tendency to focus on external causes for thoughts and feelings
- Tendency to use external (social media, TV) or internal (fantasy, daydreaming) distractors to escape

What are some signs this state is activated in your body?

How did this state help you survive? How and when does it continue to be helpful?

How is this state making life difficult for you? How is it not aligned with the deepest wants and needs of your authentic Self?

Freeze or Dissociate State

- Habit of disconnecting from your physical body to find safety
- Tendency to feel detached from yourself and your emotions
- Tendency to perceive the world around you as distorted or unreal and may have a blurred or nonexistent sense of self-identity
- Difficulty recalling both short- and long-term memories

What are some signs this state is active in your body?

How did this state help you survive? How and when does it continue to be helpful?

How is this state making life difficult for you? How is it not aligned with the deepest wants and needs of your authentic Self?

Fawn State

- Habit of hypervigilance, or hyperfocus, on your external environment to find safety
- Tendency to over focus on others (*their* thoughts, feelings, or behaviors)
- Tendency to over focus on outcomes or external validation

What are some signs this state is active in your body?

How did this state help you survive? How and when does it continue to be helpful?

How is this state making life difficult for you? How is it not aligned with the deepest wants and needs of your authentic Self?

Now that you have gained a better understanding of your nervous system responses or states, spend the next few days (or weeks) witnessing yourself and begin to explore your coping habits using the following questions. Write down your reflections in the space below or in your chosen notebook:

How often and under what circumstances (or when) do you tend to distract yourself by picking up your phone to scroll, turning on the TV, or keeping yourself endlessly busy with tasks?

How often and under what circumstances (or when) do you tend to consume food or other substances?

How often and under what circumstances (or when) do you find yourself checking out entirely, unsure of where your attention even is?

How often and under what circumstances (or when) do you tend to distract yourself by thinking about the past (replaying events that have already happened) or worrying about the future (imagining what could happen or all of the things you could be doing)?

How often and under what circumstances (or when) do you find yourself imagining things as different than they actually are?

How often and under what circumstances (or when) do you find yourself worrying about other people's needs or experiences?

How often and under what circumstances (or when) do you find yourself focusing more on the outcome of activities instead of appreciating or engaging with the process of doing the activity?

I f you're like me, you're learning that your body has existed in a dysregulated state for a long time. I spent most of my adult life in a dysregulated state, and I have some great news—you can bring your nervous system back into balance and create safety in your body. We can help our body come back into balance by supporting its needs (please continue to use the Wellness Check-In on page 57 as you complete this section). When you consistently address your body's overall physical needs, you increase its ability to cope with and tolerate stress and other emotions.

In addition to supporting your needs for nutrients, sleep, and movement/rest, we are going to practice some exercises that help send signals of safety to the body. Try practicing each of the following exercises daily.

Physiological Sigh

This breathing pattern in which two inhales through the nose are followed by an extended exhale through the mouth helps to calm the nervous system. The back-to-back inhales help to reinflate the tiny air sacs within our lungs, otherwise known as the alveoli. The alveoli naturally deflate during our normal breathing patterns and when this happens, our oxygen level decreases and our carbon dioxide level increases. This signals stress to our body. Practicing a physiological sigh allows the alveoli to reinflate, taking in more oxygen and rebalancing oxygen and carbon dioxide levels, sending signals of safety to your body.

- Inhale through the nose two times, one right after the other.
- Exhale through the mouth, extending your exhale longer than your usual breathing pattern (think the length of a yawn).
- Notice the feeling of calm or relief within your body (i.e., less tension in your shoulders, relaxation of your facial muscles, etc.) upon exhaling.
- Repeat.

Muscle Relaxation
(Through Tension and Release)

This is a practice where you tense a group of muscles as you breathe in, and completely relax the muscle group all at once as you breathe out. You can work through each muscle group of your body in any order or use the sequence listed below. One of the ways our body responds to anxiety and stress is with muscle tension. This muscle relaxation practice helps release this tension, allowing your body to relax into safety.

Refer to the following chart that includes a helpful how-to for each muscle group or experiment with what works best for you. Repeat the following steps:

1. Find a safe, quiet space where you're comfortable and are able to lie down.
2. Breathe in and tense the muscle group (tightly but not to the point of pain or cramping) for four to ten seconds.
3. Breathe out and completely relax the muscle group all at once (do not relax it gradually).
4. Relax for ten to twenty seconds before moving onto the next muscle group. Notice the difference between how the muscles feel when they are tense and how they feel when they are relaxed.
5. Repeat steps 1–3 on the next muscle group until you have worked through every muscle group.

FOREHEAD AROUND EYES AND NOSE CHEEKS AND JAW	Scrunch your face by closing your eyes and lips tightly. Bring your forehead and lips into an exaggerated frown. Clench your jaw.
SHOULDERS NECK UPPER BACK	Shrug your shoulders tightly up to your ears and touch your chin to your chest.
WRISTS FOREARMS HANDS	Clench your fists tightly into a ball, curling your wrists inward to create tension in your forearms.
CHEST STOMACH	Tightly curl your upper body inward (like you are in the fetal position), tightening the muscles in your chest and stomach.
HIPS GLUTES UPPER THIGHS	Tightly clench the muscles in your glutes, hips, and upper thighs (quadriceps).
LOWER LEGS FEET	Tightly clench the muscles in your calves and feet (maybe bending your toes to create a ball-like shape with your feet).

Expanded Range of Eye Motion

Our eyes send messages to our brain, letting it know if our body is safe or unsafe. When we feel stressed or unsafe, our focus narrows as we scan our environment looking for the possible threat. Our eyes may even begin to make quick, rapid, darting movements in this threat state. When we expand our range of sight and gently scan the horizon line or a point farther out in distance, our brain receives the message that we are safe enough to do so. Here's an exercise you can use to signal to your brain that your body is safe:

1. Find a safe, quiet space where you're able to sit or stand comfortably.
2. Focus on your two pointer fingers, extend your arms directly out in front of you, keeping your head straight forward and your eyes focused on your fingertips.
3. Focus your eyes on your left fingertip.
4. Keeping your head straight and immobile, move your left finger in a diagonal motion up to the left and back to center, following it with your eyes only.
5. Repeat this practice (head straight, following your left finger with your eyes) as you now move it directly out to the left (middle) and back to center.
6. Repeat once more, now following your left finger as you move it in a diagonal motion down to the left and back to center.
7. Now switch to your right hand and repeat steps 4–6 on the right side, moving your finger up to right (diagonal), out to the right (middle), and down to the right (diagonal).
8. Notice how your body feels. Do you feel calmer or more at peace? The greater the range of eye motion we have, the safer our body feels.

**Expand Your Range of
Eye Motion Exercise**

ARE YOUR PHONE HABITS *Stressing You Out?*

Many of you spend most, if not all, of your days engaged with some type of technological device—a computer, phone, or tablet. Looking at these small, illuminated screens for too long is not only unnatural to humans (who have evolved with more access to expanded visual cues like the horizon line), but it can also activate a stress response. Just staring at these devices stresses the body, and the content you may consume can have its own impact.

Begin to notice how you feel after using your phone or other devices for an extended period of time. Practice taking breaks from this narrowed visual focus to allow your eyes to expand their focus into the outer limits of your field of vision (known as the *periphery*, or what's above, below, and to either side of you). Simply look up and away from your phone into the distance every few minutes to stimulate a calming effect in your nervous system.

Self-Soothing Touch

Gentle, soothing touch activates the vagus nerve, helping us feel calm, comforted, and safe. Like being cuddled, this physical gesture of warmth and care soothes distressed emotions and provides a feeling of physical security.

- Find a place to lie or sit comfortably for the next few moments. If you feel safe to do so, you may choose to close your eyes.
- Gently place both hands on your chest, over your heart.
- Notice the feeling of warmth and gentle pressure of your hands, feeling your own touch upon your body.
- Take two or three deep inhales, feeling the natural rise and fall of your chest as you breathe in and out.
- Feel the energy between your hands and heart as you move your hands in a small circular direction over your heart.
- Notice the warmth and the energy swirling beneath your hands. Imagine a golden light swirling around your heart space beneath your hands.
- Remain here for a few breaths, noticing the sensations in your body. You may stay here for as long as you'd like.

Bilateral Brain Stimulation

Bilateral stimulation refers to practices that activate the two hemispheres, or right and left sides, of the brain, using visual, auditory, or tactile stimuli. This stimulation helps decrease our body's physiological arousal and stress response, resulting in a feeling of calm and increased attentional flexibility (less preoccupation with stress-inducing thoughts).

There are three ways to stimulate bilateral brain communication:

1. **VISUAL OR EYE MOVEMENT:** Follow a moving object back and forth across your perceptual field. Grab a pen or pencil (or any other item) and hold it with an outstretched arm directly in front of your chest. Focus your eyes on the tip of the item as you begin to move it slowly to the left and right of your visual field, following its movement without turning your head by moving only your eyes.

2. **AUDITORY OR SOUND STIMULATION:** Listening to specific binaural or solfeggio audio tones can stimulate our brain in calming ways. Both binaural beats and solfeggio frequencies can be found online (e.g., Google, YouTube, etc.) or through different music apps (e.g., Spotify, Apple Music, etc.). Each will have different effects (e.g., sleep, focus, creativity, etc.) and can be used throughout the day accordingly to stimulate your desired brain state.

   • **BINAURAL BEATS:** An auditory phenomenon is created by our brain when we listen to two tones with slightly different frequencies in each ear at the same time (when listening through a headset/headphones). The *binaural beat* is the third, or combined, tone that is then perceived by the brain. These beats have been found to decrease feelings of stress, anxiety, or other physiological arousal and can even synchronize our brain waves when used consistently over time.

   • **SOLFEGGIO FREQUENCIES:** Specific ancient tones or sound frequencies can stimulate the brain and help promote different mental or physical responses. Different frequencies enhance different states (calm/sleep, creativity, etc.) in the body.

3. **TACTILE OR KINESTHETIC CUES (I.E., SELF-TAPPING):** Manually touching alternating sides of your body can bilaterally stimulate your brain. A few ways to do this are:

- While sitting, standing, or lying comfortably, place your right hand on your left shoulder and your left hand on your right shoulder. Gently alternate tapping or grabbing each shoulder in a consistent rhythm or pattern.
- While sitting, standing, or lying comfortably, gently tap or squeeze each of your upper thighs/legs in an alternating and consistent rhythm or patter.
- While sitting, standing, or lying comfortably and with both feet grounded, gently tap each foot on the ground in an alternating and consistent rhythm or pattern.

Sensory Safety

Our senses are useful and easily accessible tools for relieving stress and helping our nervous system return to a balanced state. Below you'll find a suggestion for how to utilize each of your senses to create presence and safety in the body. There are many different ways to use each sense. You might start with the ideas below and discover your own sensory habits that feel soothing. Find out what works for you and write it down so you can access these feel-better prompts anytime you need them.

- SIGHT: Take a look at pictures of someone you care about or of a place that helps you feel calm (like a picture of a loved one or nature). Focus your attention on how you *feel* when looking at these images.
- SMELL: Light a scented candle, use an essential oil diffuser, or burn some incense and take in the aromas—lavender, rosemary, and jasmine can all be calming.
- TOUCH: Wrap yourself in a soft, warm blanket or feel the earth beneath your bare feet or under your hands. Draw yourself a warm bath and allow your body to soak in it for a few minutes.
- TASTE: Slowly suck on some herbal candy or sip on some herbal (chamomile, lavender, etc.) tea, noticing and savoring the flavors that fill your mouth.
- SOUND: Play your favorite soothing music or find a space outside where you can tune in to the soundtrack of nature (e.g., the whispers of the wind or birds around you).
- MOVEMENT: Engage in any rhythmic or repetitive movement (e.g., knitting, walking, biking, swimming, etc.) to help calm the body. However you choose to move your body, focus your attention on your changing and calming physical sensations.

MY SENSORY PLAN FOR WHEN I'M STRESSED

Sight:

Smell:

Touch:

Taste:

Sound:

Movement:

BODY-CONSCIOUS PAUSE

N ow that you are becoming aware of your connection to your physical body, let's practice living more consistently *in* your body. One way to do this is to integrate body-conscious pauses throughout your day. By checking in with your body before making any choice to engage in physical self-care (i.e., eating, resting, moving) you will increase your connection to your body and its physical needs.

My body-conscious pause comes when I first get out of bed. I do some deep stretches and take some breaths into my belly as I wake my body up from its stiff sleep state. You can set an alarm throughout the day to remind you to intentionally pause and check in with your physical body. In this moment, make the choice to fully shift your attention to the *experience of being in your body* and exploring the physical sensations present. Use the following space to write down and take note of your experience as you begin. You may find it helpful to repeat this list on an additional piece of paper (or anywhere you can access it throughout the day), reminding you to pause and intentionally connect with your body's physical experience.

Body pause: (time)

Physical experience/sensations present:

Body pause: (time)

Physical experience/sensations present:

Body pause: (time)

Physical experience/sensations present:

Body pause: (time)

Physical experience/sensations present:

Body pause: (time)

Physical experience/sensations present:

RESISTANCE TO
Change

These body conscious check-ins can bring up discomfort because, as you begin to pay more attention to your physical body, you may become conscious of feelings you have suppressed or avoided for many years.

If you notice resistance as you connect with your physical body, begin to practice shifting your thoughts to acknowledge the challenge and view it in a more positive light. For example, instead of thinking, "This is too hard," you might think, "This is new and unfamiliar." Instead of thinking, "I'm never going to like my body," you might think, "I'm learning a new relationship with my body and am doing the best I can right now."

Begin to use body-conscious pauses throughout your day to become aware of your body's physical needs. Your body sends signals when its needs (nutrients, movement/rest, oxygen) are being met or unmet. Learning these different cues will help you respond to your body more consciously and intentionally.

Nutrients

Nutrients are essential to life and are necessary for our body to survive, function, grow, and reproduce (if we choose to).

Create a habit of using the body-conscious pause on pages 75–76 throughout the day to observe the various changes in your energy levels and nutritional needs. As you pause, ask yourself:

Do I feel energetic and alert?

Does my body need nutrients—Am I feeling hungry and need to refuel?

Is my body satisfied—Am I feeling full so I can stop eating?

Using the questions below, spend time witnessing and reflecting on your consumption patterns. Remember, the goal is simply to be a curious, objective, and honest witness to yourself.

How do you decide when you'll eat? A particular time of day (i.e., when it's "lunch" or "dinner time")? When your stomach feels hungry? As a distraction from uncomfortable emotions?

How conscious are you when you eat? Do you actively choose what you'll consume or eat whatever's available or offered?

Are you present to how your food tastes when you're eating it?

Do you stop often to check in with your body while you're eating to notice if it's becoming full or satisfied?

Do you stop to check in and notice how your body feels after you eat?

PHYSICAL VERSUS EMOTIONAL HUNGER

Many of us eat for reasons other than our body's actual hunger level or its need for nutrients. As you begin to witness your eating habits, you may notice, like I did, that you eat or focus on food as a way to soothe or distract yourself from uncomfortable emotions. Take a look at the chart below and begin to consider the various reasons why you choose to eat.

PHYSICAL HUNGER	EMOTIONAL HUNGER
I eat to replenish my body's nutrients.	I eat to avoid/distract from certain feelings or to feel a different way.
My hunger arises gradually, in waves, and I don't feel an urgent need to eat immediately.	My hunger happens suddenly, overtaking me and making me feel like I need to eat immediately.
My body indicates its need to eat by a growling stomach or hunger pangs, which usually occur a few hours after my last snack or meal.	My body usually indicates emotional upset or stress, which can occur at random times throughout the day or night.
I am open to different types of foods to satisfy my hunger.	I usually have intense cravings for a specific food, taste, or texture.
I am able to consciously eat my food, actually tasting and savoring each bite.	I am often not paying attention when I'm eating, or I am shoveling food quickly into my mouth without actually tasting it.
I can feel satisfied and am able to stop eating when I feel full.	I often don't feel satisfied and am unable to notice or stop eating even when I'm full or my body is physically uncomfortable.
I feel replenished and don't experience regret, guilt, shame, or self-loathing after eating.	I often feel guilty, regretful, shameful, or self-loathing after eating.

Conscious Eating Journal

Keeping a journal of your food choices and your feelings in relation to them—why you chose a certain food and how it makes you feel—can be a helpful tool in witnessing your eating habits. On the following page, you will find a blank Conscious Eating Journal template that you can photocopy or transcribe into your notebook. Spend the next few days (or weeks) noting how you feel when you eat.

Note: This exercise is intended to be an objective practice of witnessing why and how you eat, not a practice to log calories or judge food choices. If you have a history of dysfunctional eating and wish to modify or skip this exercise, please feel free to do so.

As you assess your hunger and fullness in your journal on a scale of 1-5, keep in mind the following guidelines:

HUNGER 1: starving, dizzy, lightheaded; 2: no energy, possibly feeling irritable, emptiness in stomach and a strong urge to eat; 3: little energy, starting to feel emptiness in stomach and an urge to eat; 4: energized and little urge to eat; 5: no urge to eat
SATIETY OR FULLNESS 1: just starting to feel satisfied; 2: fully satisfied; 3: may be able to eat a few more bites but don't need food for fuel; 4: starting to feel discomfort from fullness; body feels too full and physically uncomfortable

CONSCIOUS EATING *Practice*

If, like most of us, you begin to witness that you are not fully conscious and are feeling distracted or rushed when you eat, it will be helpful to begin the following practice:

- Set a daily intention to spend a conscious moment with your body, assessing its nutritional needs before you eat, asking what it wants, and stopping often throughout your consumption to continue assessing its satiation or fullness.
- Set a daily intention to practice pausing a moment before you eat to visualize the ingredients that are a part of your meal, noting how your body feels as you picture each ingredient.
- Set a daily intention to practice eating more consciously by paying attention to how the food feels and tastes as you chew it. Savor the different tastes and textures.

CONSCIOUS EATING JOURNAL

BEFORE (WHAT ARE YOU THINKING/ FEELING/ DOING?)	HUNGER SCALE (1–5)	FOOD CHOICES	SATIETY OR FULLNESS SCALE (1–5)	AFTER (WHAT DO YOU THINK/FEEL NEXT?)

Movement/Rest

Movement and rest are essential to allow our body (including our brain) to replenish and repair. Create a habit of using the body-conscious pause on pages 75–76 consistently throughout your day to explore your body's energetic needs:

ENERGY LEVEL

- Overall, is your body's energy feeling full and expansive? Do you have the necessary resources to cope with your day (including any stress or other emotions you may encounter)?
- Overall, is your body's energy feeling depleted? Do you need to rest a bit to recharge?
- Overall, is your body's energy feeling nervous or agitated? Do you need to move a bit to release some tension?
- Do you pay attention to your body's energy throughout the day, noticing its shifts and changes?
- What typically causes noticeable shifts or changes in your body's energy? How does your body's energy feel when you are thinking about the past? The future? The present?

ENERGY FLOW

- Overall, does your energy feel balanced, flowing through your body?
- Do any areas of your body feel constricted, tense or agitated (your muscles or joints)? Do you need to do some stretching or other releasing activity?
- Do any areas of your body feel exhausted or achy (your legs or feet)? Do you need to do a calming activity like taking an Epsom salt bath or laying down?
- Do you pay attention to your body's energy flow throughout the day, noticing any shifts and changes in its overall state?

CONSCIOUS MOVEMENT *Practice*

If, like most of us, you notice that you're not fully conscious of your body's energetic needs, begin to:

- Set a daily intention to practice connecting with your body to assess its energetic resources and its needs for movement or rest.

- Set a daily intention to practice connecting with your body when moving to witness changes in your energy (i.e., noticing when your energy feels depleted, replenished, shifted, or released).

Body Energy and Stress

- Your body consists of energy and matter (e.g., cells, organs, muscles, fascia), helping create your experience of physically moving through the world. Fascia, or the elastic connective tissue that runs throughout your body, plays an important role in how you navigate the world. Tight fascia not only constricts physical energy and movement (causing chronic aches in the body, joints, or head) ,it also sends signals of stress to the brain. Repetitive movements or overuse, a lack of overall activity (e.g., caused by sitting or standing for long periods), poor posture, and stress all lead to tension and pain in our bodies and minds.
- If you spend most of your time in one position throughout the day, begin to take breaks to move your body in a different way (by switching positions or getting up to take a walk). If you notice areas of tension or stuckness in your body's energy or fascia system, practice releasing this constriction through tools such as:
    - Stretching, yoga (yin), myofascial release or foam rolling, acupressure, acupuncture, or trigger-point therapy, Tai chi, qigong, Reiki , Tapping or emotional freedom technique.

Every cell in our body needs oxygen to function and cope with the stress of daily life. As we've been learning, stress actually changes our body's natural rhythm of breath, sending signals to our mind that we are under threat. Create a habit of using the body-conscious pause on pages 75–76 consistently throughout your day to connect with your breath to explore your body's stress level and resources:

Overall, is your breath calm, slow, and coming from deep in your belly? Is your breath quickened and coming from your chest? Is your breath barely perceptible or are you holding it?

Do you notice changes in your breathing in response to stressful experiences in your external environment (scary or worrying events) or internal environment (stressful thoughts about the past, present, or future)?

CONSCIOUS BREATHING

Practice

Stress (and other emotions) can get trapped in our body and often manifest in our breathing patterns. Begin to practice taking a conscious moment with your body to assess its current stress level and to use your breath to regulate when needed.

- Set a daily intention to practice connecting with your breath to assess your body's current stress level by noticing where your breath feels restricted or stuck.

- Set a daily intention to notice how your breathing changes in response to different experiences (e.g., watching or reading the news, social media, etc.) and begin to limit attention to stressful or activating content.

- Set a daily intention to begin to practice slow, deep breaths to regulate your nervous system when you notice activation (quickened, shallow, or constricted breathing).

Practice

As you are working through these exercises, you are hopefully becoming more aware of how you speak about, think about, and treat your physical body. You may begin to witness just how often you criticize, shame, or compare your body to others. Each of our bodies is a living miracle that manages our digestion, breathing, and heartbeat without a conscious thought, yet few of us appreciate all of the hard work our bodies do to support us every day.

Body appreciation is the act of consciously focusing on our physical bodies with emotion of gratitude. The following body-appreciation exercise offers a powerful way to reconnect to your body. Of course, difficult emotions are going to arise. Some of you may even feel like you want to stop or like you're going to cry. For many of you, this may be the very first (*and only*) time you've ever showed your body appreciation, and that can feel intense. Practice allowing any feelings or thoughts to surface without judgment.

When you witness any internal criticism of your body, remember, this voice isn't *you*. Practice seeing these critical moments as an opportunity for you to begin to change very old habits by learning to speak to yourself in new, healthy ways.

Let's begin.

Body-Appreciation Visualization

1. Find a comfortable and safe place to sit or lie for a few minutes and allow your body to settle into the present moment. If you feel safe to do so, you may choose to close your eyes to limit external distractions and help you focus on your internal world of sensations.

2. Take three deep breaths, feeling your belly expand with air as you relax into the peace of the sensation.

3. Bring your attention to the top of your head and neck. Spend a moment or two sensing this area of your body that carries your brain. Notice your mind feels wise, containing all of your life's experiences. Take a moment to thank your brain for the wisdom it stores.

4. Bring your attention to your chest. Spend a moment or two sensing this area of your body that carries your heart. Notice your heart feels open to receiving and giving love, allowing you to connect with the world around you. Take a moment to thank your heart for the wisdom it stores.

5. Bring your attention to your stomach and hips. Spend a moment or two sensing this area of your body that nourishes and supports you daily. Notice your stomach and hips feel strong, allowing them to be your foundation. Take a moment to thank your stomach and hips for the wisdom they store.

6. Bring your attention to your legs and feet. Spend a moment or two sensing this area of your body that moves you around daily. Notice your legs feel powerful and flexible, allowing you to journey about your life. Take a moment to thank your legs and feet for the wisdom they store.

POWER OF
Belief

Beliefs are practiced thoughts that have accumulated through and been confirmed by years of lived experience. Most of your beliefs were created in childhood, stored in your subconscious mind, and repeated over time, eventually becoming neural pathways etched into your brain. Once in your subconscious, your beliefs became a filter for all of your current and future experiences. Thankfully, just as these beliefs were formed with repetition, we can begin to create new ones by consistently practicing new thoughts each day.

If you struggle with negative or uncomfortable thoughts about your body, it's important to practice affirmations for body self-empowerment and love. Repeating these new thoughts consistently will, over time, help you begin to love and accept your body even if you don't think you can.

Affirmations

for Body Empowerment and Love

Here are some affirmations to help you begin to change the way you think about your body. Remember, in order to harness the power of neuroplasticity, you will want to repeat these affirmations every day, especially if you initially find them difficult to believe. You may want to write them down and place them in areas where you are sure to see them often. The more exposure your brain has to this new messaging, the better.

My body is strong and capable.

I am safe in my body.

My body is intuitively wise.

Every day my body is healing.

When I move my body, I also move through stressful emotions.

I appreciate my body.

I know my body is working hard for me every day.

I give my body respect and rest, and I consciously care for it.

I am conscious of when my body needs rest or needs me to push through.

I'm safe to feel the sensations within my body.

When my body feel stressed, I breathe deeply and slowly.

I know how I can make my body feel safe.

My body is a unique gift.

I am at peace with my body.

I am grateful for my body and the way it helps me experience life.

My body is whole, complete, and beautiful.

I am worthy of taking care of my body and its needs.

Nothing about my body is shameful, and I openly accept it.

I forgive myself for any way I treated my body in the past.

Transform Your Habit Self

I created the Future Self Journal tool for my own healing journey and offer it as a free resource for the SelfHealers community. It's been downloaded over 500,000 times and I've received thousands of letters from people who've changed their lives by using it every day. I still use this tool, and it's had a profound impact on my life. The Future Self Journal is based on the power of neuroplasticity, the brain's ability to change or create new neural pathways throughout life. When used consistently, this practice will allow you to break free from your subconscious autopilot—or the daily conditioned habits that are keeping you stuck.

You can begin to move forward by engaging in the following activities:

- Observing the ways you remain stuck in your past conditioning (as we will continue to explore throughout this workbook)
- Setting a conscious daily intention to change
- Setting small, actionable steps that support daily choices aligned with a new and different future
- Following through with these new daily choices despite the common and universal presence of mental resistance

Pick one category from the Wellness Check-in on page 57 (i.e., nutrients, movement/rest, sleep, or stress) for which you want to cultivate a new habit that better honors your physical needs.

Set an intention to keep one small promise to yourself every day that can help you meet this goal and better align your body's physical needs with your daily choices.

Complete the following journal prompts (or create a similar one of your own) every day using your new intention to help you keep that promise and form a new habit.

Today I am **conscious of my body when I'm eating.**

I am grateful **for another opportunity to explore being conscious with my body.**

Change in this area allows me to feel **more aware of my body's sensations around fullness.**

Today I am practicing **when I am conscious of my body's changing sensations during mealtimes.**

Today I am _____.

I am grateful for_____.

Change in this area allows me to feel_____.

Today I am practicing when_____.

Using this journaling practice daily, we can change aspects of our self-care habits that don't meet our body's unique requirements, one at a time. Remember, consistency is important to create a new habit. Consistency means practicing our new choice regularly, so it becomes a part of our everyday routine. New habits may take weeks or months to stick, depending on your personal journey, but that journey always starts by keeping one small daily promise. That's how true transformation occurs.

It's time for you to celebrate yourself because you've done some very deep work in section two. Now we are ready to continue along our journey to meet our emotional self.

AFTER PRACTICING THE EXERCISES IN SECTION TWO, YOU'LL KNOW HOW TO

Understand the connection between your body and mind

Understand how to use mind-body tools to heal

Understand your nervous system's role in wellness

Safely return to your body by regulating your nervous system

MEET YOUR EMOTIONAL SELF

DRIVEN BY EMOTION

WHAT YOU'LL LEARN

How the conditioned mind is formed

What your ego is and its role in your daily life

What your core beliefs are and how they affect you

How cycles of emotional addiction are created

Our emotions have a profound effect on how we experience the world around us. Our mind and body are interconnected, creating our emotional experience. Emotions are felt in the body through sensations, and in the mind as thoughts or feelings. Fear in the body might feel like tightness in the chest or as an extra or agitated energy throughout your arms or legs, causing you to fidget. Fear in the mind might come through as hypotheticals (or "what if" thoughts) or worst-case scenarios replaying certain thoughts over and over again.

This journey to understand your emotional self will be powerful. You're going to discover that most of what you think, feel, and do is a reflection of your past conditioning and not a reflection of who you actually *are*. This conditioning creates the emotions we live through daily, so let's dive in.

YOUR CONDITIONED MIND

Our conditioning exists within our subconscious mind, and it holds all the stories about who we think we are. Our conditioned mind is habitual, meaning we continue to think the same thoughts, feel the same feelings, and react in the same way each day. As you will remember from our discussion of neuroplasticity (page 33), the more we continue these patterns, the more we fire the same neural networks in the brain. Over time, we fired these neural networks so frequently they became cemented (or *habitual*), resulting in the autopilot that runs our conditioned mind.

The conditioned mind impacts how we view ourselves and others. Beginning at birth, when our brain was still developing, everything we heard and saw was being absorbed into our subconscious. As we soaked in the world around us, we were learning social cues, language, and lots of other information.

As children we didn't have the mental or emotional maturity or ability to fully make sense of our world. We were in a developmental state (called *egocentrism*) where we personalized everything we experienced. *What we or others did meant something about who we are.* Those of us who had a parent-figure with a very demanding job or who engaged in addictive behaviors and therefore wasn't able to spend time with us may have internalized a belief that they are not "worthy of getting that parent's time or attention." With this developmental immaturity, even if a parent explained to us that they were doing the best they could to support a family or was using substances to try to self-regulate, we struggled to make sense of their absence.

Those of us who had a parent-figure who was harsh, critical, or who consistently fell into cycles of rage may have formed a belief that we were "bad and deserving of punishment." With time and repetition of these cycles, we may have come to internalize the belief that we are flawed, unworthy, or that something is "wrong" with us. Without the emotional maturity to see things from a wider perspective that comes with experience, we may develop damaging beliefs that persist throughout our lives.

I can assure you that nothing is "wrong" with you. In fact, you might not yet be aware of many of your most beautiful aspects. You've made a powerful choice to unlearn the beliefs that you've inherited to learn the truth of *who you are.*

Your Ego Protects Your Conditioned Mind

Our mind constantly creates meaning to make sense of the world around us. For example, if we meet someone we are interested in and we don't immediately hear from them, we might assume that "they're not interested in us." Or, if we are passed up for a job opportunity, we might assume that it's because the employers think "we're an unqualified imposter." The more frequently we make these assumptions or assign these meanings to our experiences, the more these interpretations form into a cohesive narrative or story line that accompanies us throughout life. These stories make up our *ego* (we will go into more detail on this shortly), or simply, the story of us. Based on the sum of our lived experiences, our ego solidifies into our idea of *who we think we are.*

Our ego then continues to filter information into our consciousness that matches the beliefs of our conditioned mind. If our conditioned mind believes that we are not worthy, our ego will filter all our experiences through that belief. That means that any time we begin to explore a new relationship, for example, despite any perceived chemistry, our thoughts may begin to race with concerns (*Did I say something wrong? Did I insult them? Did I talk too much about x?*) when we don't hear back from them. These *ego stories*, or assigned meaning to our experiences, are examples of the different ways our mind tries its best to navigate uncertainty. Uncertainty feels unsafe to the mind. Our conditioned mind relies on the certainty of known and previously "confirmed" beliefs (*I'm not worthy of my parent's time or attention*) in order to help us feel safe.

You might be asking yourself, *why would my ego create and maintain a story that's hurtful?* The answer is: a hurtful *why* will always be more appealing than an uncertain reality. You have likely noticed that people rarely, if ever, respond to questions they don't know the answer to with *I don't know* and instead usually reason their way through an answer. The human mind craves certainty and drives our ego to work tirelessly to confirm and reinforce the stories we've repeated since we were young.

The beliefs that live in our subconscious mind affect our physical experience, too. As we focus on the emotional feeling of rejection for not being "good enough," our nervous system responds to this perceived threat and our hearts may begin to race, our breath may quicken, and our muscles may tense. The longer our nervous system stays dysregulated, the more our mind and body begin to react to each other, and the emotional and physical discomfort that results can feel overwhelming. We may cope with this discomfort in ways we later regret, like "obsessively" monitoring social media accounts or dating apps. For many of us, this physiological cycle leads to emotional addiction, which we will discuss in more detail on page 157.

MEET YOUR EMOTIONAL SELF

We have so many beliefs, we could never be aware of them all. They're stored within our subconscious mind, and most of those beliefs were formed before we were consciously able to choose them. We inherited them as children from the people that were closest to us—our parent-figures and close family, school systems, childhood friendships, community members, religious and cultural institutions, and media. These are called our core beliefs, and our brain works consistently to confirm them, ultimately creating the reality we experience every day.

Our ego is highly protective of our core beliefs and when these beliefs are challenged, it often responds with emotional reactivity. For many of us, this results in us yelling in defense of our beliefs when we hear from someone who disagrees, or completely avoiding interacting with others who hold different beliefs.

Because our ego associates our beliefs with our *identity*, even a relatively minor challenge can trigger a full-body nervous system response. To put it simply, beliefs that challenge our identity feel like a threat to *who we are*. This is why it's critical to understand that we are not our beliefs. Through curiosity, openness, and a willingness to communicate with those who challenge us, we can begin to identify the beliefs that actually align with our true values.

YOUR MIND'S *Filter*

Every day, your brain is bombarded with stimulation from the environment around you. Because you would become overwhelmed tending to all of this information, a part of your brain called the reticular activating system (RAS) unconsciously filters out all unnecessary information so that only the important stuff gets through. A quick example of the RAS at work is hearing *your* name spoken by people at the table next to you in a crowded, noisy room. Your beliefs are one of the common filters used by your RAS to determine what's meaningful to you. Your subconscious uses the RAS to confirm its most deeply held beliefs, even if they no longer align for you. What this means is that if you secretly think you're an imposter at your job, you will only see more instances to confirm that belief in your daily work life.

Begin to consciously identify and witness the most commonly held beliefs using the exploratory questions that follow.

WHAT ARE YOUR CORE BELIEFS?

T his exercise will help you explore and identify the different core beliefs that may be living in your subconscious mind. Some of our core beliefs are grounded in experiences that were difficult, challenging and/or painful. These uncomfortable or difficult experiences—and the emotions they bring up—are not new. They've rested deep in your subconscious until now. This act of consciously exploring and witnessing your core beliefs will lift the veil to painful past experiences that your mind has worked to bury. It's necessary to remain objective and compassionate with yourself as you go through these exercises.

RACE AND ETHNICITY

What comes to mind when you think about *race* and *ethnicity*? How connected are you to your race or ethnicity? What beliefs do you carry about those who look similar to you? What beliefs do you carry about those who don't look like you?

_____

_____

RELIGION OR SPIRITUALITY

What comes to mind when you think about *religion* or *spirituality*? What are your predominant views on religion? What does your connection (or non-connection) to a higher power (e.g., God, Higher Power, Source, the Universe) mean for you?

_____

_____

RELATIONSHIPS

What comes to mind when you think about relationships and their purpose? What comes to mind when you think about different *roles* in relationships? What do you think your role should be in relationships?

_____

_____

GENDER

What comes to mind when you think about gender and what it means to you? What roles do you think you should take on given your gender? What gender roles did you see your parents take on?

_____

_____

FEELINGS

Are there certain feelings you think are okay to express? Are there certain feelings you think are not okay to express?

_____

_____

MONEY

What comes to mind when you think about money? What does money mean to you? What have you been told about money?

_____

_____

VOCATION/PURPOSE

What comes to mind when you think about work, your job, or your career? How, if at all, do you think your deeper passion or purpose is connected to your idea of work or your work experience?

_____

_____

WORLDVIEW

What do you think about the world—is it a safe or unsafe place? Is it just or unjust? Do you think you can make an impact or do you think your actions are meaningless?

_____

_____

SEXUALITY OR PHYSICAL AFFECTION

What comes to mind when you think about sexuality and physical affection or contact? What comes to mind when you think about sex or other sexual activities?

_____

_____

BEAUTY IDEALS

What comes to mind when you think about *beauty* or an ideal physical look? What messages about physical appearance were you given from parent-figures and other loved ones?

_____

_____

DO YOUR BELIEFS MATCH YOUR BEHAVIOR?

When our ego is involved, we tend not to see our behavior accurately. This is a protective mechanism, and it blocks us from being able to change. You might have heard someone reference that another person is *in denial*. This is exactly what the ego does, it keeps us unconscious to the reality of ourselves. In order to see yourself, you have to look past the ego and all the stories it creates. Some people call this *awakening*. And it's definitely not an easy process. As we awaken or see the reality of who we really are, and the role we play in our reality, we can begin to exist with integrity and meaning; our beliefs and actions can align.

This next exercise will help you determine whether your words and actions are in alignment. Most of us can identify inconsistencies between what we believe and how we behave. This is common and is not something to be ashamed of. Once we identify these inconsistencies and become more concrete in our true beliefs, we can begin to act in ways that reflect our beliefs.

Race and ethnicity beliefs (*from pages 97–98*):

_____

_____

My behavior: How do you act around others who look similar to you? How do you treat them? How do you act around others who look different than you?

_____

_____

DO MY BELIEFS AND MY BEHAVIORS ALIGN?

Religious or spiritual beliefs (*from pages 97–98*):

_____

_____

My behavior: What role does religion or spirituality (e.g., God, a Higher Power, Source, the Universe) play in your day-to-day life?

_____

_____

DO MY BELIEFS AND MY BEHAVIORS ALIGN?

Relationship beliefs (*from pages 97–98*):

_____

_____

My behavior: How do you experience your relationships? What roles do you play in your relationships? How do you feel playing these roles?

_____

_____

DO MY BELIEFS AND MY BEHAVIORS ALIGN?

Gender-based beliefs (*from pages 97–98*):

_____

_____

My behavior: What do you allow yourself to do because of your gender? What do you not do because of your gender?

_____

_____

DO MY BELIEFS AND MY BEHAVIORS ALIGN?

Beliefs about feelings (*from pages 97–98*):

_____

_____

My behavior: What feelings do you allow yourself to have? What feelings do you not allow yourself to have?

_____

_____

DO MY BELIEFS AND MY BEHAVIORS ALIGN?

Money beliefs (*from pages 97–98*):

_____

_____

My behavior: What role does money play in your life? How do you spend your money? Are you comfortable talking about money and receiving it?

_____

_____

DO MY BELIEFS AND MY BEHAVIORS ALIGN?

Beliefs about vocation/purpose (*from pages 97-98*):

_____

_____

My behavior: What is the role of work, your job, or your career in your life? How, if at all, is your deeper passion or purpose connected to your work?

_____

_____

DO MY BELIEFS AND MY BEHAVIORS ALIGN?

Worldview (*from pages 97–98*):

_____

_____

My behavior: How do you experience the world overall—do you feel safe and able to trust the happenings of the world around you? Do you feel powerless and unable to trust the world around you?

_____

_____

DO MY BELIEFS AND MY BEHAVIORS ALIGN?

Beliefs about sexuality or physical affection (*from pages 97–98*):

_____

_____

My behavior: Are you comfortable thinking about or talking about sex? Are you comfortable with close physical contact?

_____

_____

YES   NO   NOT SURE

Beliefs about beauty and physical appearance (*from pages 97–98*):

_____

_____

My behavior: Are you comfortable and secure with your physical appearance? In what ways do you change your physical appearance to meet your ideals?

_____

_____

DO MY BELIEFS AND MY BEHAVIORS ALIGN?

YES   NO   NOT SURE

MEET YOUR EMOTIONAL SELF

MEET YOUR INNER CHILD

Now that we're gaining clarity on some of the conditioned beliefs that may be coloring our experiences, we can dive a bit deeper into our subconscious mind. The inner child is the part of our subconscious where we carry our unmet childhood needs, suppressed emotions, connections, imagination, creativity, intuition, and ability to play. It is also where we carry the wounding from shameful and traumatizing past experiences. Almost all of us have experienced shameful or overwhelming events (or many events) in childhood that have created deep wounds. As we've grown into adults, those wounds don't just disappear; they're carried by our inner child. It's these wounds, or unresolved emotional experiences, that created and continue to contribute to many of our subconscious behaviors today.

Our inner child needs to be seen, heard, and acknowledged—to simply be who they are. For many people I've worked with just having an awareness that an inner child exists within them can change the way they speak to themselves. We didn't have the choice or ability to protect ourselves in certain situations as children. No child brings on, deserves, or allows abuse, ever. As adults, we each have the opportunity—and responsibility—to begin acknowledging the wounded inner child within us. It is our job to become our own wise, loving inner parent that can begin meeting and nurturing the core needs that were not consistently met in childhood. We can begin doing so only after we have taken the time to meet and acknowledge our inner child's existence, as well as understand their core needs.

On the opposite page you will find a chart that lists your inner child's core needs and can help you determine if they were met or unmet. Before we explore further, I want to acknowledge that for some people the thought or idea of engaging with their inner child feels uncomfortable. I know that when I first did this work, it felt awkward and I had to overcome a lot of mental resistance. Additionally, if you've endured abuse or neglect, it may not feel safe to connect with your inner child. I'll remind you again to take breaks as you need them, and always remember you can do these exercises with a therapist if it feels too overwhelming to do them alone.

When our inner child's core needs aren't consistently met, a wound is created, and that pain endures. The chart on the opposite page details some of the qualities of a wounded inner child compared with a nurtured inner child. Spend some time considering the feelings and behaviors that come up consistently for you, and how they might be tied to inner child wounds.

INNER-CHILD CORE NEEDS

IDENTITY/SIGNIFICANCE IN THE WORLD	Sense of self or awareness of who I am Felt connectedness to family and community
SAFETY	Sense of safety to fully express yourself Sense of trust within relationships
CONNECTION/LOVE	Emotional bond that comes from vulnerable sharing and sense of secure connection
AUTONOMY	Freedom to choose what is best for one's self, without pressure, force, or cohesion
VARIETY/STIMULATION	Desire to learn, see, and experience new things Sense of openness and receptivity
GROWTH	Willingness to face challenges in order to learn and grow (or evolve) from experience

QUALITIES OF A WOUNDED AND NURTURED INNER CHILD

WOUNDED INNER CHILD	NURTURED INNER CHILD OR *AUTHENTIC SELF*
Feels unsafe	Feels safe
Blames or criticizes (self and others); acts defensively	Observes self without judgment and allows authentic expression (self and others)
Compares self to others (looking for *external validation*)	Validates self internally
Engages in limited or fear-based thinking (e.g., "I am not enough" or "There is not enough")	Access to limitless or safety-based thinking (e.g., "There is opportunity and possibility in every moment")
Overreacts or shuts down (i.e., silent treatment or dissociation)	Open to play, imagination, and creativity (e.g., painting, writing, drawing, etc.)
Engages in black-and-white thinking (i.e., absolutes of "right" and "wrong")	Open to multiple perspectives or interpretations
Neglects or harms oneself	Practices disciplined self-care (moving and resting when needed)
Lacks boundaries (self and others)	Honors boundaries (self and others)

INNER-CHILD JOURNAL

L et's now begin to practice observing and acknowledging the presence and influence of your inner child in your daily life:

- Observe your inner child throughout the day. Use the chart on page 105 to help guide you.
- Find a safe, quiet space where you feel comfortable and have little to no distraction.
- Reflect and journal your responses to the following prompts. Use the space provided or copy this format into your notebook.

EXPERIENCE

What happens to activate my inner-child wound? (Use the previous Qualities of a Wounded and a Nurtured Inner Child tables for guidance.)

_____

_____

THOUGHTS

When my wounded inner child is active, what am I thinking?

_____

_____

FEELINGS

When my wounded inner child is active, what am I feeling? (Focus on sensations.)

_____

_____

REACTIONS

When my wounded inner child is active, how do I react? (e.g., tantruming, sulking, detaching, etc.)

_____

_____

THE SEVEN INNER-CHILD ARCHETYPES

When we were younger, most of us had access to a childlike part of ourselves that was free, filled with wonder and awe, and connected to the inner wisdom of our authentic Self. Over time and as a result of our experiences and conditioning, most of us began to disown or deny these authentic parts in order to play roles that helped us receive the love that was available. The following list details the common inner-child archetypes that reflect various inner-child patterns. Read through the descriptions and spend some time witnessing your inner child's conditioned roles.

- **THE CARETAKER.** Gains a sense of identity and self-worth through neglecting one's own needs. Believes that the only way to receive love is by taking care of or tending to others.
- **THE OVERACHIEVER.** Feels seen, heard, and valued through success and achievement. Uses external validation as a way to cope with low self-worth. Believes that the only way to receive love is through performance.
- **THE UNDERACHIEVER.** Keeps themselves small, unseen, and beneath their potential due to fear of criticism or shame about failure and often takes themselves out of the game (or quits) before it's even played. Believes that the only way to receive love is to stay invisible and unnoticed.
- **THE RESCUER/PROTECTOR.** Views others as helpless, incapable, and dependent and derives their love and self-worth from being in a position of power by attempting to rescue others around them in times of need. Believes that the only way to receive love is to take away others' problems.
- **THE LIFE OF THE PARTY.** Presents as happy, cheerful, or comedic and never shows pain, weakness, or vulnerability. Believes that the only way to receive love is to make sure that they and those around them are happy.
- **THE YES PERSON.** Drops everything and neglects their needs in the service of *all* the wants and needs of others. Like the caretaker, they were often modeled self-sacrifice. Believes that the only way to receive love is to be selfless.
- **THE HERO WORSHIPER.** Constantly looks to a person or guru to follow, much like in childhood when a parent-figure (or other caretaker) was perceived as superhuman, without faults. Believes that the only way to receive love is to reject their own needs, desires, and intuition and views others as a model for learning how to live.

Neuroscience has proven that writing down your thoughts by hand strengthens cognitive skills and supports neuroplasticity. Over time, the building of these neural pathways allows us to rewire our thoughts, feelings, behaviors, and reactions. Writing a letter to your inner child from the voice of a loving, wise inner parent can be a helpful way to begin nurturing and healing the wounded inner child within.

Find a safe, quiet space where you feel comfortable and have little to no distraction.

If you can, find a photo of yourself or picture yourself at age three through seven. Take a look at this photo or mental image and ask yourself:

- What is it I would like to tell my child self?
- What did my child self need to know or hear but was never told?
- If I could go back in time and offer encouragement, love, or support to my child self, what would I say?

Now, start using these prompts to write a letter to your child self. Allow it to be as long or as short as you want; just let it flow. Some of you may even write this letter using your non-dominant hand, which can help you tap into this younger part of yourself. It's common to cry or feel intense emotions as you do this, just allow the emotional release. Remember to use the Building Your Own Internal Support System resources you created on page 5 and have hopefully been practicing consistently throughout your journey thus far. If you find this practice therapeutic, you can continue writing these letters to yourself and see how they change over time.

Dear Little Wounded/Hurt [insert your name],

_____

_____

_____

_____

_____

_____

Meet Your Inner Child Guided Meditation

MEET YOUR INNER CRITIC

E ach of us has an inner critic that judges and shames ourselves or others. No one is harder on us than we are on ourselves. Rather than lifting us up and supporting us, our inner critic is the voice that focuses on judgment and negativity, viewing ourselves or others and our lives through a lens of difficulty, failure, and dissatisfaction. I've found in my experience that if we had critical parent-figures the inner critic can be more intense, more harsh, and more present.

While our inner critic may sound harmful, its existence is actually adaptive. Once we understand its origins, we can appreciate its purpose. Like our ego, it protects us from uncertainty. Anything new is unfamiliar, and anything unfamiliar signals threat. The voice of our inner critic reminds us of our potential pain, our fears, and disappointments we've experienced.

A highly active inner critic can take a toll on one's emotional and physical well-being. When we take a moment to understand why we have an inner critic, we begin cultivating awareness of what it is saying and become empowered to create new inner dialogue. Using the following chart, take some time over the next few days or weeks to begin to identify your inner critic:

MY INNER CRITIC EXAMPLE

EVENT/EXPERIENCE	INNER CRITIC MESSAGE
I answered a question incorrectly (at work or school) and my peers or colleagues laughed at me.	I'm not smart; I can't get anything right.
I don't look like the model I see in a magazine or on TV.	I'm ugly; I'm unattractive.
My partner didn't put the dishes away like I asked them to.	They're inconsiderate; they ignored my request on purpose.
My co-worker messed up something on a report.	They're incompetent; I'm the only one who can do things correctly.

MY INNER CRITIC

EVENT/EXPERIENCE	INNER CRITIC MESSAGE

SOFT AND LOVING *Eyes*

When we feel critical, judgmental, or negative, our field of vision becomes smaller and more focused (usually on our imperfections). Many of us consistently look at our physical body with these critical and judgmental eyes. This narrowed vision communicates a message of stress or threat to our body.

When looking at yourself in a mirror, take a moment to soften your gaze, and bring your eyes into a neutral state:

- Relax the muscles around your eyes and face. Let your gaze soften.
- Allow a softer, gentler, loving feeling to wash over you.
- Check in with your body and notice any shifts or changes in your body's sensations of stress and tension.

Your Wise Inner Parent

Our wise inner parent is the nurturing, encouraging, and comforting voice that our inner child may not have always (or ever) received. As adults, we can become our own wise inner parent, beginning the process of meeting our inner child's unmet needs. Use the following table as reference in discovering how your wise inner parent would speak to your inner child.

EVENT/EXPERIENCE	INNER-CHILD WOUNDING	WISE INNER-PARENT VOICE
Felt criticized or shamed over behavior	*I'm rejected.* *I'm not lovable.*	*My behavior does not determine how lovable I am.*
Passed over for job, reward, etc.	*I'm unworthy.* *_____is better than me.*	*Achievements do not affect my value or worthiness.*
Ghosted by a new friend or love interest	*I'll never be chosen.* *I'll be alone forever.*	*I may never know why this person is unavailable, and their behavior does not reflect who I am.*
Excluded from social plans or an event	*I'm not accepted.* *_____ doesn't like me.*	*Not getting invited places does not necessarily mean I am not liked. People with interests that align with mine will include me.*
Did something mistakenly or by accident (e.g., spilling food or breaking something)	*I can't do anything right.*	*Things don't always go as planned or as I'd like them to.*

Wise Inner-Parent
Affirmations

Our wise inner parent is always within us; we just might not know how to access them. We can begin to create an ongoing dialogue with our wise inner parent by practicing the following affirmations. By consistently using these affirmations, we can begin to lay down new neural pathways that we can access the next time our inner child needs some support.

I recently used one of these affirmations when I was running late for an appointment. Sitting in the car judging myself for being late, I could feel my body begin to tense as my heart started racing. My inability to control the traffic around me was increasing my stress and making me feel more anxious. Remembering that my inner child was likely also feeling scared in that moment, I took a deep breath and said, "You are safe." I felt calmer after offering this support to myself rather than being in a cycle of self-shame.

Here are some affirmations to use to begin to access your own wise inner parent:

You are safe, and I'm going to take care of you now.

You are worthy of love and belonging.

You are lovable just as you are without performing or achieving.

It's okay to ask for what you need and want.

You can feel any way you want to feel. There is no such thing as wrong or right emotions.

Your needs matter.

You are worthy and have unique gifts waiting to be expressed.

You are allowed to take the time to feel your feelings.

Making mistakes is a natural part of life and you can learn from them.

You are allowed to not know all of the answers.

You can play and explore just because you want to.

You are allowed to say "no" to the people, places, and things that don't serve you.

You deserve to take the time for self-care.

Reparenting Your Inner Child

Reparenting is the process of actually learning how to meet the needs of your inner child that were not met in childhood. It is the practice of *becoming* your own wise inner parent through daily self-care and observation, giving ourselves the nurture we may not have received in childhood.

You'll Know You Need Reparenting If

- You have a habit of self-betrayal or not keeping your word to yourself.
- You hold low self-worth.
- You have dysfunctional relationship dynamics.
- You hold a chronic fear of criticism.
- You have issues setting and holding boundaries.
- You have a lack of understanding of your own needs, wants, desires, and passions.

THE FOUR PILLARS OF REPARENTING

LOVING DISCIPLINE

As children, many of us were not taught simple, helpful, healthy habits and rituals. We can begin to cultivate loving discipline by:

. . . .

Keeping small promises to ourselves

Developing daily rituals/routines

Saying no to things that do not serve us

Holding boundaries even when we are uncomfortable

Disconnecting and spending time in self-reflection

Clearly stating our needs in objective (non-judgmental) language

SELF-CARE

As children, many of us were not taught the value of sleep, movement/rest, nutrients, and connection to nature. We can cultivate this self-care by:

. . . .

Going to bed a bit earlier than usual

Cooking/eating a home-cooked meal

Meditating for five minutes (or longer)

Moving our body for five minutes (or longer)

Journaling

Spending time in and connecting with nature

Allowing the sun to touch our skin

Reaching out to and connecting with someone we love

JOY

As children, many of us were not taught the value of joy in spontaneity, imagination, creativity, play, and pure presence. We can cultivate this joy by:

. . . .

Dancing or singing freely

Doing something unplanned

Finding a new hobby or interest

Listening to our favorite music

Complimenting a stranger

Doing something we absolutely loved as a child

Connecting with friends and loved ones

EMOTIONAL REGULATION

As children, many of us were not taught the value or practice of having emotional awareness. We can begin cultivating emotional regulation by:

. . . .

Observing how emotions feel in our body

Noticing what causes our nervous system responses to activate

Witnessing emotional responses without judgment; allowing any and all emotions to pass through us while simply observing

Practicing intentional breathing (see examples on page 6)

Co-regulating with a loved one or pet

Cold therapy

MEET YOUR EGO

Ego Work

The ego tends to get a bad rap. Some people see the ego as a negative quality or a character flaw. But as you've learned, every human has an *ego*, or the part of the mind that holds the *identity* of who we believe we are, who we believe others are, and what we believe about the world. It's helpful to think of our ego as a collection of the stories that we've inherited from childhood. While many people villainize the ego, it is a necessary part of the human psyche that helps make sense of who we are as we experience life. It's when we are unaware of the ego that it can drive our life experiences and cause problems. What we actually want to do is *soften* or *integrate the ego*, allowing us to witness it and make conscious choices beyond its instinctive reactions.

Most of us are unconscious of our ego and don't even know it exists. Picture this: You get into your car, and instead of sitting in the driver's seat, you sit in the passenger's seat blindfolded. In the driver's seat is your ego driving as fast as it wants, taking you wherever it chooses. This is how many people live their lives. What we want to do is take off our blindfold and get back into the driver's seat. We want our ego to sit next to us, as a passenger on our journey. From time to time, our ego will pop up (typically when we are most afraid) and try to gain control of the steering wheel. Because we are aware of this, and we commit to practicing ego work, we simply see the ego and guide it gently back to its seat. The more we do this, the more we become empowered and gain control of our lives.

Ego work is a way to separate yourself from your ego and create space to make choices in alignment with our authentic Self. This exercise will allow you to detach from all of your ego stories and view yourself in a new, empowered way.

Before you begin you're going to want to name your ego. Choose a name for your ego that feels right. In my community, people have a ton of fun giving their ego all sorts of names, so be creative. I've named my ego Jessica. And let me tell you, sometimes Jessica has a mind of her own!

I will name my ego:

_____

Congrats! Your ego has a name and you are in this very moment *not* your ego. Now, let's practice ego work.

I AM EXERCISE

Set a timer for two to five minutes and begin to explore and write all the thoughts that arise when you ask yourself the question *Who am I?* Note anything and everything that comes to mind (this is called *free association*), including *all* of the things that you identify with, that resonate with you, and that you love or care about.

_____

_____

_____

_____

Spend the next few days (or weeks) witnessing yourself throughout your day, noticing any and all instances when you think or say the words "I am . . ." Note what words, descriptors, or aspects of your identity most consistently come next.

Typical ways I think about myself throughout the day:

_____

_____

_____

_____

Typical ways I describe myself to others throughout the day:

_____

_____

_____

_____

WITNESS YOUR EGO IN ACTION

Now that we are beginning to gain a better understanding of how our ego thinks about us, let's practice witnessing our ego in action throughout the day. Using the following prompts, take the next few days (or weeks) to witness and explore how and when your ego appears. For example: *Who are you typically interacting with? What are you typically doing? How are you typically feeling?*

Think of the most recent time someone disagreed with your beliefs or opinions. How did you feel and how did you react?

_____

_____

_____

When you hear a new belief or idea you aren't familiar with, how do you typically react? (Do you feel open? Shut-down? Overwhelmed?)

_____

_____

_____

Think of a recent time when someone came to you with an issue they were struggling with. Did you bring the conversation back to yourself or your own issues (saying things like "I would never" or "If I were you, I would . . .") or were you able to actively listen without inserting your own perspective?

_____

_____

_____

How often and under what circumstances do you think or say things like "I should be doing x" when you're doing something else?

_____

_____

_____

How often and under what circumstances do you do things to appear a specific way to people in your daily life or on social media (e.g., taking a vacation for Instagram photos, taking a job because it will give you social validation, buying a house that is financially stressful to impress friends)?

_____

_____

_____

When someone gives you feedback on something and you feel uncomfortable, how do you typically react? Do you become defensive? Do you take deep breaths and try to listen to the information? Do you shut down and spiral into critical self-talk?

_____

_____

_____

When you make a common mistake (like being late for a meeting, losing your temper, or forgetting to run an errand), how do you typically speak to yourself? Do you think or say things like "I'm such an idiot"? "I deserve to be fired"? "I never get anything right"?

_____

_____

_____

When you try something that is unfamiliar or new to you and it feels uncomfortable, how do you react? Are you able to work through the "I'm not good at this" stage to keep trying?

_____

_____

_____

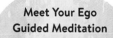

**Meet Your Ego
Guided Meditation**

Here are the most common ego stories that I've seen within my community. You might identify with one right away, or you may identify with a couple of different stories. Take the next few days (or weeks) to witness these stories as they arise throughout your day. This will help you to witness the consistent stories your ego creates based around your daily experiences.

HELPLESSNESS OR CODEPENDENCY

Hyperfocus on one's need to be in a relationship in order to be happy or fulfilled. Tendency to care for other's needs and no awareness of any difference between "us" or our needs and another or "their" needs. May include themes of incompetence, inadequacy, or constant negative comparison to peers or others.

How often and under what circumstances (or when) do you think about checking in with others before checking in with yourself to make a choice?

_____

_____

How often and under what circumstances (or when) do you think about needing others?

_____

_____

WORTHLESSNESS, SHAME, OR ISOLATION

Themes of feeling shameful in public (based on physical appearance or social behaviors) or private (based on our hidden desires). Hypersensitivity to perceived criticism, rejection, or blame. Often includes thoughts about being alone in the world, being different from others, and/or not part of any group or community as a result of your "defects."

How often and under what circumstances (or when) do you think you are unlovable or alone because of shameful aspects of yourself?

_____

_____

How often and under what circumstances (or when) do you think about how different or separate you are from others around you?

_____

_____

NEGATIVITY OR PESSIMISM

An excessive focus on the negative aspects of any experience or event that limits positive encounters. A sense that things that are going well will ultimately fall apart. Includes chronic worry, complaints, indecision, and hypervigilance.

How often and under what circumstances (or when) do you think about all the things that are/can go wrong, ignoring all of the things that can/are going right?

_____

_____

How often and under what circumstances (or when) do you think about your current issues in life?

_____

_____

UNLOVABILITY AND APPROVAL- OR ACHIEVEMENT-SEEKING

Excessive emphasis on need for approval and validation. May include a hyperfocus on status, appearance, social popularity, money, or achievement in order to gain attention from others.

How often and under what circumstances (or when) do you think or worry about what others are perceiving about you?

_____

_____

How often and under what circumstances (or when) do you think or worry about the feedback you're getting in different areas of life?

_____

_____

PERFECTIONISM

Hyperfocus on and criticism of the behavior(s) of self and others. A belief in punishment for mistakes and unmet expectations. Rigid narratives that do not allow for human imperfection or empathizing with others' feelings. Includes unrealistically high moral, ethical, cultural, and religious standards.

How often and under what circumstances (or when) do you think about your performance or behaviors?

_____

_____

How often and under what circumstances (or when) do you think about the morals behind your (or others') actions, feel like a fraud/ imposter, or worry your mistakes or flaws will be found out?

_____

_____

SELF-SACRIFICE

A tendency to put others' needs or emotions before one's own in order to maintain connection or to avoid feeling selfish. Hyperfocus on the feelings, needs, or wants of others rather than one's own.

How often and under what circumstances (or when) do you think or worry about how you are being perceived in relationships?

_____

_____

How often and under what circumstances (or when) do you think or worry about meeting the needs of others before your own, even when their needs differ from yours?

_____

_____

INSECURITY OR ABANDONMENT

Patterns of instability, unreliability, chaos, or abandonment within relationships. Often worries or fears related to suffering physical or psychological harm such as health catastrophes (like a heart attack), emotional catastrophes (e.g., "going crazy") or victimization (such as robbery).

How often and under what circumstances (or when) do you think or worry about losing support in your life as a result of loved ones leaving or dying?

_____

_____

How often and under what circumstances (or when) do you think or worry about how others are showing up for you in your relationships?

_____

_____

SUPERIORITY OR ENTITLEMENT

Themes of superiority, entitlement, or privilege with a focus on one's own needs/wants without care for others. Includes feelings of competitiveness toward or domination of others.

How often and under what circumstances (or when) do you think about beating others or winning in some way?

_____

_____

How often and under what circumstances (or when) do you think that things are owed to you?

_____

_____

EMOTIONAL OVERWHELM OR SHUTDOWN

Tendency to think or worry about one's emotions or about controlling one's emotions. Can include hyperfocus on another's perceived reaction to any or all of your emotional communications.

How often and under what circumstances (or when) do you think or worry about being emotionally "out of control"?

_____

_____

How often and under what circumstances (or when) do you struggle to express your thoughts out of concern for how others will react?

_____

_____

EXPLOITATION OR VIOLATION

Patterns of hurt, abuse, humiliation, manipulation, or cheating. Can include thoughts or worries around trust or security (or connection) with others.

How often and under what circumstances (or when) do you think or worry about not getting your needs met due to another's intentional or unintentional choices?

_____

_____

How often and under what circumstances (or when) do you think about the different ways people hurt you throughout your life?

_____

_____

MEET YOUR SHADOW

Your shadow self is the part of you that you have denied or repressed since childhood. When we are children, we get all sorts of messaging from people we love about what parts of ourselves are "good" and what parts of ourselves are "bad." Many of us have felt validated when we heard praise from parent-figures who said things like, "You're such a good and polite kid for doing x, y, or z" or "Don't be x, y, or z. Share your toys."

As you've learned, when we are children, we don't have discernment about what to take personally and what not to take personally. Everything is taken literally and directly. If someone we love very much (whom our survival depends on) tells us that we are _doing_ something "bad" or "wrong," we may come to believe _we_ are _bad_ or _wrong_. For example, we might express more of our caretaking side because we have learned that part of us is _good_. We may also deny our own wants or desires, believing it is selfish to keep anything or want something just for ourselves.

All of this happens subconsciously, based on the messages we received. Sometimes, these messages are more direct, especially for those of us who were punished for having certain needs or certain emotions. For many of us, being punished for wanting a lot of attention, for crying too much, or for being "dramatic" is the beginning of adopting a persona or false self to please people around us.

Our shadow self doesn't only consist of the "negative" things about ourselves, it can also hold many positive traits that aren't socially rewarded or seen by others. Many of us are born into homes that put a lot of pressure on academic performance with hopes that this focus will result in more opportunity and a better life. Often our inherent abilities and talents that do not fit into this path are overlooked. Many of us who, as children, loved artistic expression like drawing or singing might have found these passions ignored, or may have been told to "stop messing around" or "wasting time" when we expressed ourselves in those ways. Sadly, many of our shadow selves include creative talents that were not socially rewarded or were dismissed completely.

When we aren't aware of our shadow self, we tend to project it onto other people. We are quick to judge others and use labels (e.g. *arrogant, entitled, greedy*). You'll notice that the traits you project onto others tend to be patterns that you see in other people consistently. It may surprise some of you to hear that these traits are also within yourself, which is why you see them in others. Sometimes, we may even identify ourselves as "better" than those people, or we may virtue signal when we're around them to cope with the internal conflict of not accepting those aspects of ourselves. The truth is that *all* of us contain messy, broken, hurt, selfish, and jealous parts, and this doesn't make us "bad." The more we accept *all* parts of ourselves, the more we can accept *all* parts of others.

We can be just as quick to project "good" traits onto others. We may even "hero worship," or see some people as larger than life or perfect. The reality is, even the people we admire have flaws, insecurities, and qualities that cause them to feel shame. It's also important to understand the "good" traits that we admire and see within others are *also* within ourselves, which is why we see them in others. It's only through doing the inner work that we can begin to actually see the good we overlook.

Like our ego, our shadow self is ultimately looking to be integrated, or simply to *be seen*, acknowledged, and honored, so that we can become complete. In other words, so that we can be our whole, fully expressed, authentic Self. Many parts of you have been dismissed or subjectively seen as "bad" by people based on their opinions. In our shadow self lie the creative, beautiful parts of ourselves, as well as the parts we're afraid of (e.g., the vengeful parts, the jealous parts, the fearful parts, and all of the sometimes scary thoughts that come with them). Meeting our shadow self is meeting our true humanity, and we can all learn to love it.

DO YOU FEEL
Shameful or Guilty?

While some of you may be using these terms interchangeably, shame and guilt are two different feelings. Guilt is a feeling we have when we believe we have *done* something wrong, usually with our actions or inactions. Shame is what we feel when we believe *we* are inherently wrong or worthless. While both of these feelings have evolutionary (and social) value by indicating awareness of how we (and our actions) impact others and the world around us, shame erodes our sense of self and can often result in secretiveness around our undesirable choices.

Begin to notice when you are feeling shame and practice separating yourself from your choices or actions. Reframe your thoughts to indicate that *you* are still worthy and lovable, even if you (or others) feel disappointed with your actions.

SHADOW WORK:
MEET YOUR SHADOW

Spend some time exploring the following questions. Some of these answers might not come to you right away, and that's okay. You can always bookmark this page and come back to it. The more open you are to this work, the clearer the answers will become.

What do you think are some of the worst traits, characteristics, or behaviors a person can have?

_____

_____

_____

What traits, characteristics, or behaviors don't you like about yourself?

_____

_____

_____

What trait(s) do you see in people that you notice yourself always feeling envious of (or wish you had)?

_____

_____

_____

What are you most proud of or what do you feel is your greatest accomplishment?

_____

_____

_____

What do you believe this accomplishment means about you?

_____

_____

_____

If ever there was a time when you were young and felt badly about yourself (stupid, foolish, or embarrassed), what happened? What did you think about yourself? How did you feel?

_____

_____

_____

What do you think about failure or making mistakes? How do you feel when you fail or make a mistake? Do you accept failure and mistakes as part of life or do you feel yourself consumed by fears of them?

_____

_____

_____

What traits, characteristics, or behaviors make you feel the most insecure?

_____

_____

_____

If ever there was a time when you were young, when people commented on aspects of you that were "wrong," "bad," "negative," or that you should change, what did they say? How did you feel?

_____

_____

_____

Do you find yourself still trying to change these aspects of yourself today?

_____

_____

_____

What traits, characteristics, or behaviors did your parent-figures idealize, or think and speak highly of, when you were a child? Did they idealize money or success? Work ethic? Having nice material things? Being "strong" or "not weak"? High achievement or good grades? Self-sacrifice or being "selfless"?

_____

_____

_____

What traits, characteristics, or behaviors do you idealize? How do you attempt to meet these idealized standards?

_____

_____

_____

How easily did you "fit in" growing up—or how accepted or rejected did you feel by your peers or friends? How did you feel? Why did you imagine you were being accepted or rejected?

_____

_____

_____

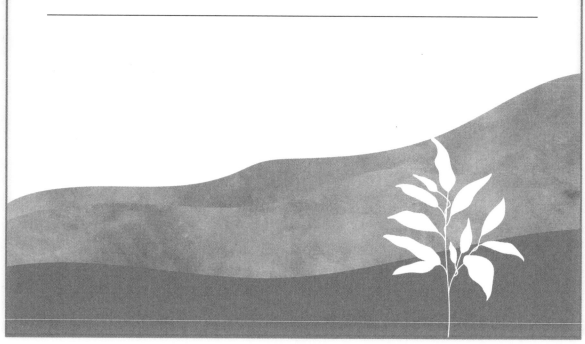

SHADOW WORK:
WITNESS YOUR SHADOW IN ACTION

We can see our shadow through others and our daily interactions with them. Noticing the thoughts that come up when we are around friends, family, and strangers will allow us to discover parts of ourselves that we haven't yet seen. We can also notice what comes up when we consume information through social media, television, or movies. Doing this will cause a profound shift in your life because most of us unconsciously take in information or interact with the world around us. It's through conscious reflection on these experiences that we gain a deeper awareness of their influence and meaning.

The behavior we engage in often has an emotional payoff. Usually, our behavior is based in a desire to satisfy an unmet need. Typically, this motivation is unconscious, and we are not aware of why we do the things we do. In this exercise we are going to work on becoming conscious of our unconscious motives.

I mostly consume content about _____ and the emotional payoff I get is feeling _____.

In my closest relationships, we usually are bonding over _____ and the emotional payoff is feeling _____.

When I post on social media, I'm usually posting things about _____ and the emotional payoff is feeling _____.

When I am alone, I usually think about _____ and the emotional payoff is feeling _____.

When I talk negatively about someone, I'm usually talking about _____ and the emotional payoff is feeling_____.

Now, let's look at your answers. You'll probably notice a pattern. *Are you feeling justified, angry, morally superior, or "less than" others?* None of these feelings are wrong or bad, we all have them.

Once we get past judging ourselves, we can take a kinder look at why we are acting as we are.

Why might I be engaging in these patterns? What is it about myself that I may be struggling to accept, love, or acknowledge?

_____

_____

_____

Meditation for Wholeness

Expand Your Limits

Limiting beliefs are inherited in childhood and practiced throughout adulthood. Limiting beliefs can keep us stuck, repeating cycles without us even being aware of them. In order to become aware of our limiting beliefs, let's first look at the three most common categories they tend to fall into.

Three Types of Limiting Beliefs

1. **Limiting beliefs about who you are:** these are beliefs about yourself that make you feel as if there are things you cannot do because something is "wrong" with or "missing" within you. Common limiting beliefs about yourself include: *Some things are out of my reach;* and *There is something inherently wrong or different about me.*

2. **Limiting beliefs about other people:** these are beliefs about people that create a sense of powerlessness for ourselves. Common limiting beliefs about others include: *People are always out to get me; no one will ever love me;* and *I can't ask others for help.*

3. **Limiting beliefs about the world:** these are beliefs about the world around you that impact your ability to reach your goals or aspirations. Common limiting beliefs about the world include: *There is not enough for me to have what I want;* and *There is not enough time to do what I want.*

LIMITING BELIEF CHECKLIST

Take a look at the Limiting Belief Checklist and spend some time exploring which ones may be most active for you:

_____ I am only worthy of love if I am taking care of someone.

_____ My achievements define my success.

_____ People are always out to hurt me.

_____ I believe I have no control over the outcome of my life.

_____ My self-worth is defined by what I achieve.

_____ I often judge myself, criticize myself, or believe that I'm just not good enough.

_____ I often try to make people change, even when they don't want to.

_____ I feel powerless to change my life.

_____ I believe that I'm lacking what it takes to heal or transform my life.

Now that you've uncovered some of your limiting beliefs, you will want to begin to unlearn them. We all have limiting beliefs (usually many of them) and our first step in unlearning is to recognize that our beliefs are just practiced thoughts and are not necessarily true. When working on releasing limiting beliefs, we don't want to judge ourselves for them or try to talk ourselves out of them (this can actually make the beliefs stronger).

We want to create new, empowering belief reframes. Through empowering belief reframes, we can begin to adopt new beliefs that tell a different story than the one we have been repeating about ourselves, other people, and the world around us. When we practice these reframes, you'll notice that they do two things:

1. They acknowledge what is out of our control. Remember, things happen to us that we have zero control over for reasons we cannot or may never understand.

2. They acknowledge what we do have control over. In most situations, there is something that we can control, including the meaning we assign to our experience, our reaction to it, or how we speak about it.

EMPOWERING BELIEF REFRAMES

ick a consistent limiting belief from the Limiting Belief Checklist (or after witnessing one of your own) to begin to reframe.

LIMITING BELIEF: People are always out to hurt me.

ROOT OF BELIEF OR PAST EXPERIENCE: The way my dad treated me.

EMPOWERING REFRAME OR WHAT I DO HAVE CONTROL OVER: The way I treat myself.

Here are some examples of how to use empowering reframes to change old, limiting beliefs:

I didn't have control over (my root of belief or past experience) and I do have control over (what I can do now).

I didn't have control over (the way my dad treated me) and I do have control over (how I treat myself).

I didn't have control over (how I felt when I made that mistake) and I do have control over (being kind to myself after making the mistake).

I didn't have control over (how my mom talked about my body when I was growing up) and I do have control over (how I speak about my body today).

Now you will want to begin to practice this on your own:

I didn't have control over _____ and I do have control over _____ .

I didn't have control over _____ and I do have control over _____ .

I didn't have control over _____ and I do have control over _____ .

I didn't have control over _____ and I do have control over _____ .

Biased Brain

Your survival and evolution have benefited from your brain's habit of prioritizing "negative" stimuli around you. Noticing and attending to any possible threat in your surroundings as quickly as possible has allowed you to move out of harm's way. This is called the negativity bias and it is something all human brains share. We filter the world through a lens that is attuned to threat.

Begin to witness your limiting beliefs using the Limiting Belief Checklist on page 131 to explore how they may be impacting your daily perceptions, keeping both your body and mind stuck in its old habits. Using the Empowering Belief Reframes exercise on page 132, practice new, more empowering thoughts to change your core mindset, beliefs, and ultimately daily actions.

MEET YOUR EMOTIONS

motions are our main way of interacting with the environment around us. They are evolutionarily designed signals to help us identify what's most important to safely navigate our surroundings. They manifest as physiological sensations (e.g., changes to our body's heart rate, breathing patterns, muscular tension, and neurotransmitters or hormones) that give us information on how we're experiencing the present moment: *Are we in an unsafe situation? Do we have a need that's currently unmet?*

While *emotions* are associated with bodily reactions that include nervous system activation, neurotransmitters, and hormones, *feelings* are the conscious experience of these physiological reactions. Because survival is determined by our moment-to-moment experiences, our brain attempts to interpret what's happening around us as quickly as possible so we can spring into action if, and when, we perceive a threat to our safety. To interpret what's happening and decrease the discomfort of uncertainty, our subconscious mind assigns meaning to all our daily experiences. Our brain then uses this meaning to interpret our body's physiological changes (or *emotions*), resulting in the different *feelings* we have.

WHAT'S GOING ON AROUND YOU?

Your sensory experience of your environment

+

WHAT'S HAPPENING IN YOUR BODY?

Emotion or body sensations (interoception or *inner-sensing*)

+

HOW YOUR SUBCONSCIOUS IS MAKING SENSE OF WHAT'S HAPPENING (OUTSIDE AND INSIDE)?

Assigned meaning based on past experience

=

FEELING

EXAMPLE:

WHAT'S GOING ON AROUND YOU?

I'm hearing my partner yell loudly.

+

WHAT'S HAPPENING IN YOUR BODY?

I startle and sense my heart rate increase.

+

HOW YOUR SUBCONSCIOUS IS MAKING SENSE OF WHAT'S HAPPENING
(OUTSIDE AND INSIDE)?

My partner must be upset because they're yelling.

=

FEELING FEAR

WHAT'S GOING ON AROUND YOU?

I don't see a text response from a friend.

+

WHAT'S HAPPENING IN YOUR BODY?

I sense my face and body getting red and heated.

+

HOW YOUR SUBCONSCIOUS IS MAKING SENSE OF WHAT'S HAPPENING
(OUTSIDE AND INSIDE)?

My friend must be ignoring me.

=

FEELING HURT
(MAYBE ANGER)

90-SECOND RULE OF *Emotions*

As physiological events, emotions typically last for about a minute and a half and eventually come to an end. When you're stressed or experiencing another emotion, your body releases cortisol and other hormones. Once the perceived stress or upsetting event has ended, your body will metabolize these hormones and your nervous system will return to its baseline state of peace and calm. Your body actually *wants* to return to this state as quickly as possible. This can only happen if your mind doesn't get in the way, as it does for many. Once emotionally activated, many of us tend to spend a lot of time *thinking* about our feelings and keeping the stress response alive in our bodies.

Begin to observe where your attention goes when you are stressed or emotionally activated. If you notice yourself getting distracted by thoughts about the upsetting event (which will only keep your body's emotional response activated), begin to practice re-focusing your attention on your breath to ground yourself back into your body.

HOW DO YOUR EMOTIONS FEEL?

Your environment is always communicating with you through your emotions, or the sensations experienced in your body. You know this to be true when you walk into a room where two people have just been fighting or there's a lot of tension. It's not always something you can put words to; it's something you feel immediately. Usually, you'll notice this same tension from the environment begin to manifest in your own body. Our bodies have an incredible way of picking up the immediate energy of a room. This communication can be extremely helpful, especially when it alerts us to pay more attention to a possibly unsafe environment, like the shivers down our spine many of us get when we enter a dark alley. Tuning in to how these internal sensations *feel* is an important step to reconnecting with our inner guidance, or our authentic Self.

While emotions are our primary way of interacting with the world, many of us aren't actually aware of how they impact our bodies. As you learned in section one, you may not be connected to or feel safe enough in your body to attune to its sensations. For those of you who still feel disconnected from or unsafe in your body, returning to the exercises in section one can help you continue to rebuild this lost connection.

We each experience emotions slightly differently, so it will be important to familiarize yourself with how *your body* registers various emotions, such as joy/happiness, anger, sadness, fear, disgust, and surprise (the core or universal human emotions). While some of you may find you tend to avoid or suppress certain emotions, it is both very normal and healthy to experience the full range of emotions. The chart below details the messages these core emotions typically send.

Take some time to witness how your body looks and feels when you're experiencing each of the core emotions.

ANGER: I notice my body begins to feel tense, my face gets hot, I clench my teeth.

SADNESS: I notice my body's energy begins to feel heavy and low, my shoulders droop, I find it difficult to smile.

FEAR: I notice my body begins to shake, my heart rate increases, my breath quickens.

JOY/HAPPINESS: I notice my body's energy begins to feel lighter, alive/active, I find it easy to smile.

DISGUST: I notice my stomach begins to clench or feel sickened, I feel like gagging, my nose begins to wrinkle.

SURPRISE: I notice my body's energy spikes quickly, and I become immediately alert, my heart rate quickens, my eyes and jaw open wider.

EMOTIONAL COMMUNICATIONS

EMOTION	MESSAGE
Anger	Boundary violation or unmet needs
Sadness	Loss
Fear	Threat to safety
Joy/Happiness	Interest, pleasure, or expansiveness
Disgust	Aversion to something offensive (physically, mentally, emotionally, or morally)
Surprise	Unexpected event or violation of expectation

Anger

_____
_____
_____

Sadness

_____
_____
_____

Fear

_____
_____
_____

Joy/Happiness

_____
_____
_____

Disgust

_____
_____
_____

Surprise

_____
_____
_____

If you have difficulty identifying what you're feeling when these sensations are actively present (in real time), take a few moments to practice the following visualization exercise for each of your core emotions:

- Find a comfortable and safe place to sit or lie for a few minutes.

- Allow your body to settle into the present moment. If you feel safe to do so, some of you may choose to close your eyes to limit external distractions and help you focus on your internal world of sensations.

- Begin to call to mind a past or imagined scenario, event, or experience where you have or can imagine feeling anger.

- Spend a few moments beginning to objectively explore the different sensations in your body as you are experiencing anger.

- If you find your attention is getting distracted by thoughts about the event or about the emotion itself (maybe by judging yourself or trying to explain or argue away how you're feeling), practice shifting your attention to your body and get curious about how it feels.

- Take a few moments to note any sensations that you noticed associated with your emotional experience of anger. Some of you may choose to also note how this visualization felt overall.

- Feel free to revisit this exercise often to continue to explore the sensations associated with anger. This can be especially helpful for those of you who are new to connecting with this emotion as you may continue to discover aspects of your experience and to also gain access to the suppressed emotions still living in your body.

- Repeat this exercise with the rest of the core emotions: sadness, fear, joy/happiness, disgust, and surprise.

- When you feel complete with this exploration, you can return your attention more fully to the room or space around you.

EMOTIONAL
Activation

A 2014 study using heat maps to examine changes in the body's physiological activity found distinct patterns for the six core emotions:

- **ANGER:** activation in upper half of body and arms; some in legs and feet
- **SADNESS:** activation in chest and head; decreased activation in arms, legs, and feet
- **FEAR:** activation in upper half of body except arms; some in feet
- **JOY/HAPPINESS:** activation throughout the entire body
- **DISGUST:** activation in upper half of body and arms
- **SURPRISE:** activation in chest and head; decreased activation in legs

Your emotions and feelings will be uniquely represented in different areas of your body, so developing your own *inner-sensing* (this is called *interoception*—more on this to come!) by exploring the different sensations will give you the foundation for emotional resilience.

YOUR RELATIONSHIP WITH
YOUR EMOTIONS

How we identify and cope with our emotions is determined both by how our emotions were tended to *within* our early relationships and how we witnessed others around us coping with their own emotions (which of course also impacts how they help us cope with ours).

In childhood, we are often overwhelmed by the responses of our nervous system and related emotions in our body. Because our brain and nervous system are *wired to connect*, we rely on others to help us regulate our body and mind through the act of *co-regulation*. If we were around others who were attuned to our emotions and who were able to help us regulate when needed, we likely felt safe enough to continue to be open to all of our emotional experiences. If our parents were overwhelmed by their own emotions and were not able to attune (or *pay attention to*) our needs, we likely shut down or closed ourselves off from some or all of our emotions.

When a baby or young child falls down and hurts themselves, they immediately begin crying. They're experiencing pain while also experiencing fear because something scary just happened that they weren't prepared for. The crying signals to the mother that her baby needs to be soothed. Babies cannot soothe their own emotions; they need an adult to show them how. Many children were raised in homes where a parent couldn't soothe their emotions. If this was the case for you, you might struggle to know what you're actually feeling or how to calm yourself down when upset. By learning to understand, process, and release your emotions, you'll feel more confident and in control of your own life.

Using the prompts on the following page, take a few moments to begin to explore the different messages you may have received from your earliest relationships.

In childhood . . .

Were emotions (including "I love yous") expressed directly in the home? If so, how were the different emotions expressed?

_____

_____

_____

Did you feel safe to express _all_ (the whole range) of your emotions in your home, or were certain emotions avoided entirely? If the latter, what emotions did you learn to avoid or dismiss?

_____

_____

_____

Was someone there for you when you were upset/in pain or in need of support? Or did you feel alone, shamed, or ignored/dismissed when you were upset/in pain or in need of support?

_____

_____

_____

Where or when may you have learned to stop yourself from expressing your emotions? Do you remember a time when you decided to stop talking to people about how you felt?

_____

_____

_____

What messages did you receive from your culture, religion, or society about emotions and emotional expression? Were certain (or all) emotions labeled as "good" or "bad," "right" or "wrong," "moral" or "immoral"?

_____

_____

_____

Did you feel like your emotions were important or unimportant? Did you feel like your emotions were accepted and explored, or did you feel they were a bother or a burden?

_____

_____

_____

For those of you who grew up with siblings or others in the home: How was conflict between family members handled in your home? Did you feel protected from being harmed by your siblings/others or did your pain feel dismissed or ignored? Were your hurtful behaviors to siblings/others dismissed or ignored?

_____

_____

_____

Did your family micromanage or try to control each other's emotions by approaching them with constant nagging, worrying, or problem solving (removing the issue to remove the emotion)?

_____

_____

_____

Did your parent-figures use substances (alcohol, drugs, food) to cope with their emotions?

_____

_____

_____

Did your parent-figures suppress or ignore their emotions in service of "martyring" themselves?

_____

_____

_____

Did you witness others taking responsibility for their emotions, or did they tend to blame their current circumstances? Did you hear things like "You made me do it" or "I wouldn't have yelled if you didn't . . ."?

_____

_____

_____

Take the next few days (or weeks) to begin to explore the impact of these early experiences by witnessing your current emotions in adulthood.

What is your current relationship with your emotions overall—do you feel all of the core emotions (happiness/joy, sadness, fear, anger, surprise, disgust)? Do you shame yourself for any or all of your emotions? Do you deny or suppress any or all emotions? If so, which ones?

_____

_____

_____

Which emotions are you most comfortable experiencing? Which ones are you most uncomfortable with or most likely to attempt to avoid?

_____

_____

_____

How present are your emotions in your relationships? How often do you talk about or share them? How do you typically respond when people (strangers, friends, family, partners) ask how you are doing or feeling?

_____

_____

_____

What kind of feedback have you received from others about your emotions? Have people commented on how often you smile or whether you frequently look upset or seem angry, sad, or stressed?

_____

_____

_____

Do you feel others interpret your emotions accurately or inaccurately?

_____

_____

_____

YOUR Inner-sensing

Even if you're unaware of or disconnected from your emotions, they are being used by your mind to create your experience of your environment (or *your feelings/reactions*). Through a process called interoception, your brain scans your bodily sensations to gauge how it's experiencing the world around you, namely to meet its needs and keep you safe.

Continue to practice reconnecting with your body using the Daily Feeling Journal so you can become more present to all of the active emotions that may be impacting your experience of the current moment.

DAILY FEELING JOURNAL

Using the body-conscious pause practice on pages 75–76, add a second check-in with your emotions. Doing so will help increase conscious awareness of your emotional experiences on a daily basis. Turn to the Feelings Wheel on page 241 if you need help identifying your emotions. The more clearly you understand how you really *feel*, the more empowered you will be to navigate these emotions in a different way.

EMOTION CHECK-IN:

What sensations are currently present in my body?

_____

_____

What am I doing or thinking (during the event or experience that's occurring)?

_____

_____

What emotions or feelings may be present?

_____

_____

HOW I COPE JOURNAL

As adults, many of us cope with our emotions as we did in childhood. If we didn't learn healthy ways to relate to our emotions when we were young, we continue to throw tantrums, pull away or disconnect from others, or act out in passive-aggressive ways (like giving the silent treatment as punishment). While we might be aware that we do these things, many of us feel like we can't stop doing them because coping mechanisms are deeply ingrained patterns that are the result of nervous system dysregulation.

Let's begin by witnessing our inner child's ways of coping by observing how we react in stressful or upsetting situations. Using the prompts associated with each example, write down your emotional reactions to any incidents that occurred recently, being as honest as you possibly can about what thoughts, feelings, and reactions you experienced at the time. In the upcoming weeks or months, if a similar incident occurs, continue to explore and jot down your reactive cycle.

Over time, you'll likely start to notice similarities in how you react to emotionally charged situations. The more you witness yourself in times of stress or upsetting incidents, the better able you'll be to identify themes that reveal your inner-child coping mechanisms. For some, this process takes weeks; for others, it takes months.

Becoming aware of your inner-child reactions and related coping mechanisms will allow you to begin to change how you respond in emotionally charged moments. For many, this means opting for responses that don't originate in childhood pain and better serve our authentic Self.

EXPERIENCE	THOUGHTS	FEELINGS	REACTIONS
What happened?	*What do you automatically think?*	*What do you automatically feel?*	*How do you automatically react?*
The position I wanted wasn't offered to me.	I'm thinking about how it wasn't fair.	I feel wronged.	I blame others.
The house chores were not completed.	I'm thinking that my partner is inconsiderate.	I feel angry.	I scream and yell.
A promised phone call from my friend didn't come.	I'm thinking that I must not matter to my friend.	I feel sad.	I withdraw and sulk.
There is a disagreement between me and a loved one.	I'm thinking about the possibility of this relationship ending.	I feel scared.	I get defensive.
EXPERIENCE	THOUGHTS	FEELINGS	REACTIONS
What happened?	*What do you automatically think?*	*What do you automatically feel?*	*How do you automatically react?*

How I Cope with Trauma and Dysregulation

As you learned in section one, the long-term effects of trauma can hijack our ability to navigate and cope with our emotions. The list below details some of the common ways many of us learned to navigate emotionally overwhelming experiences in childhood. The more we repeat these trauma responses, the more habitual these coping mechanisms can become in adulthood.

AVOIDANCE, REPRESSION, OR DENIAL: The tendency to bury painful thoughts or feelings (*If I don't talk about it, it doesn't exist*).

IDEALIZATION OR FANTASY: The tendency to exaggerate positive traits or experiences (*real* or *imagined*) rather than acknowledge objective reality. This can look like constant daydreaming about how things should be or how you'd like them to be, rather than acknowledging the reality of how they are.

INTELLECTUALIZATION OR RATIONALIZATION: The tendency to avoid feelings by thinking or analyzing your experiences (*I can think my way out of any challenge or problem*).

PROJECTION OR EXTERNALIZATION: The tendency to assume what everyone else is thinking or feeling, while denying your own similar thoughts or feelings. Or the tendency to assign blame to the external world for your thoughts and feelings (*You made me feel that way*).

DISSOCIATION OR SHUTDOWN: The tendency to separate from painful thoughts, feelings, or experiences.

SUBSTANCE USE OR OTHER ADDICTIVE BEHAVIORS: The tendency to rely on external means such as food or other substances to self-regulate through uncomfortable thoughts, feelings, and experiences.

FAWNING OR PEOPLE-PLEASING: The tendency to pay attention solely (or be *hypervigilant*) to the needs of others and the external world.

Spend some time witnessing your current emotional coping habits using the following prompts:

How often and under what circumstances (or when) do you find yourself feeling numb or avoiding your emotions/feelings entirely? How often and under what circumstances (or when) do you find yourself lying (or minimizing) to others about how you're really feeling?

_____

_____

How often and under what circumstances (or when) do you make yourself powerless to your experiences by making demands that others change or stop what they're doing so you can feel better?

_____

_____

How often and under what circumstances (or when) do you blame others for your reactive behaviors (saying things like "If you didn't . . . , I wouldn't have . . .", "You made me . . .")?

_____

_____

How often and under what circumstances (or when) do you give others the silent treatment, withhold your love by acting mean or cold, or make passive-aggressive comments?

_____

_____

How often and under what circumstances (or when) do you push away or deny your pain by turning to substances to try to feel better?

_____

_____

How often and under what circumstances (or when) do you focus on work or achievement to push away your feelings or to feel better?

_____

_____

How often and under what circumstances (or when) do you find yourself trying to explain away or rationalize your feelings?

_____

_____

How often and under what circumstances (or when) do you find yourself imagining that things are different than they are as a way to avoid how you are feeling about your current circumstances?

_____

_____

How often and under what circumstances (or when) do you find yourself worrying about what others are thinking or how others are feeling as opposed to focusing on how you feel?

_____

_____

FEEL YOUR FEELINGS

Now that we have begun to explore our habitual coping habits, we will want to create new ways to navigate our emotional experiences. When we feel comfortable actually feeling our feelings, we are less likely to need to act out or distract ourselves from feeling them.

STEP 1. WITNESS YOUR FEELINGS.

We rely on our older coping strategies and allow our inner child to become reactive when our resources are low and we can easily be overwhelmed with stress. While this is a completely normal response, our reactive behaviors are often not aligned with the needs and wants of our authentic Self.

We do this through first witnessing, accepting, and welcoming our current feelings and re-actions, without judgment. Your work here is to remain objective, loving, and kind to *all* parts of you. This is your access to creating a reality aligned with your authentic Self.

Stress Ladder

Our bodies are always communicating with us. Using this tool, you can begin practicing this first step—witnessing—by *learning* and paying attention to your body's changing cues indicating when its stress level begins to escalate. Over time, with consistent practice, this new awareness will help you understand when to pause, to take breaks, and to bring yourself back to safety.

How to use this tool:

- Get familiar with the sample stress ladder that follows and use it for reference if you'd like as you get started. You may find that you relate to many, or even all, of these cues and their positioning on the stress ladder, or you may find that your body sends cues that are not listed there.

- Practice observing yourself and your reactions throughout the day. Notice the physical sensations that occur in your body in moments of stress and escalating stress. *Where and how does overwhelm begin to show up in your body? How does stress show up in your body as it progresses?*

- Begin to write down your observations on the blank stress ladder or copy them into your notebook. Remember, witnessing becomes easier with practice. Be kind to yourself as you begin and *keep going*. Refer back to the example for more guidance.

SAMPLE STRESS LADDER

10 = I'm yelling and screaming at whoever is around.

9 = I begin to clench my hands into fists and begin pacing.

8 = My eyes narrow and I begin to turn my face into a scowl.

7 = I begin to feel my shoulders and jaw tense up.

6 = My face begins to tingle and become flushed.

5 = My breathing begins to increase and becomes louder and heavier.

4 = I feel my palms begin to get sweaty.

3 = I feel my heart rate begin to increase.

2 = I feel my stomach begin to flip or twist into knots.

1 = I'm stress free and feel calm, relaxed.

My Stress Ladder

10 = _____

9 = _____

8 = _____

7 = _____

6 = _____

5 = _____

4 = _____

3 = _____

2 = _____

1 = _____

STEP 2. ACCEPT AND WELCOME YOUR FEELINGS.

Learning to accept and welcome our feelings is a powerful act of transformation. If we were yelled at for crying, punished when we got angry, or told we were too sensitive, we adapted by detaching from those emotions all together.

Now, we are going to learn to allow whatever it is we are feeling whenever it is we are feeling it. To help you begin accepting and welcoming your feelings, we're going to practice shifting our language, or *reframing* our experiences. So many of us say things like *I am sad*, or *I am angry*, making that feeling or emotion the entirety of our experience. By doing this, many of us are keeping ourselves stuck in the feelings and repeated coping strategies and reactivity of the past.

Instead, observe yourself and your emotional reactions throughout the day. Keep a running list of what feelings come up for you and write them down using the following reframe. Use the space below or copy the prompts into your notebook:

1. **Shift your language.** Shift from "I am _____" to "A part of me feels _____."
   This helps us strengthen the reality that we are not our emotions. We are the being that is *experiencing* our emotions.
   For example: "I am <u>sad</u>" becomes "A part of me feels <u>sad</u>."

2. **Welcome the feeling.** Speak out loud, write in your journal, and practice welcoming and accepting the feeling by repeating the following:

"I welcome the feeling of _____ that I am currently witnessing/experiencing."

For example: "I welcome the feeling of sadness *that I am currently witnessing/experiencing."*

Each time you do this, practice repeating to yourself the following statement: *"I am not that emotion, part of me is* experiencing *that emotion."*

This practice gives you the opportunity to *embody* your own wise inner parent who is attuned to *all* of your feelings, empowering and nurturing both your present and future self.

STAND IN THE
Emotional Storm

As many of you are learning, emotions can be intuitive tools offering guidance on our daily journey. Having a mature relationship with our emotions means we are able to connect with these inner messengers, factoring them in when we make choices about how to cope with the present moment. One of the key habits for emotional maturity is to cultivate *equanimity*, or the ability to stand in the middle of intense emotions with a sense of mental calmness and composure. It is the practice of being with your emotions without being victim to them (*allowing them to cause overwhelm or harm to your body/mind*) or reactive to them (*allowing them to dictate your choices*).

Using the exercises on the pages that follow begin to create a new, equanimous relationship with your emotions by expanding your window of stress resilience so you can safely connect

EMOTIONAL RESILIENCE

Resilience is the ability to recover from stressful experiences. Life throws many obstacles in our path that we have little to no control over. It makes sense then, that we would all benefit from learning how to develop resilience so that we can face challenges with more grace and acceptance. In order to cultivate resilience, we have to learn how to widen our window for stress tolerance, or, put another way, we have to teach our nervous system how to deal with a wide variety of experiences.

Those of us who have endured an overwhelming past experience, or trauma, typically have a very narrow window of tolerance. Because we were overwhelmed and without adequate resources, our body's alarm system likely entered a hypervigilant, protective state. In this case, we can be emotionally triggered quite easily and feel unable to cope. Even though this state is painful for people to experience, it's actually our body's way of protecting us.

Unresolved trauma can trigger our nervous system to respond to nearly everything as if it were a threat. Of course, there is a difference between being uncomfortable and actually facing a life-or-death situation; we need to teach our bodies the difference. In order to evolve in life, we have to be able to face discomfort. Discomfort allows for growth. The more we learn to navigate what life throws at us, the more confident, secure, and at ease we can become.

The upcoming exercises are going to show you how to widen your window of tolerance and teach your body that discomfort doesn't always mean danger.

Is Your Body Keeping You Stressed?

From birth, our nervous system is *wired to connect* with others and with our environment. When we grow up in an unsafe (*physically* or *emotionally*) environment, our nervous system becomes focused on protection and survival rather than connection and engagement, impacting our openness to the world around us.

Until we create safety in our body, our stressed body and mind will keep us stuck in cycles of nervous system activation and disconnected from both our authentic Self and the world around us. Because our body and mind are connected and in constant communication with each other, a stressed body will always result in a stressed mind with racing, anxious, fearful, or panic-inducing thoughts. In simple terms, the state of our body's nervous system creates the stories we tell ourselves in our mind.

When your body is stressed, it sends a signal to your mind that your body is not safe. Your mind then responds to this signal by scanning its internal environment (*you start thinking stressful thoughts*) and external environment (*you become hypervigilant to the world around you*). If your body's energy is agitated or your nervous system is stressed out, your mind begins to race with stressful thoughts about the past or future.

Using the signs of nervous system activation listed below, spend the next few days (or weeks) beginning to witness your body's reaction to stress. Its posture and energy flow are a product of the state of your nervous system; reflect on how this state then affects your attention (or *presence*) and experiences in the current moment.

Fight

- Squared-off shoulders and puffed-out chest
- Flexed muscles
- Increased rate and volume of speech
- Fidgety or spastic movement

Flight

- Shrunken body (to look smaller), tucked or hunched shoulders
- Standing in the background or slinking off
- Decreased volume of voice
- Distracted eye movements

Freeze/Shut Down

- Head hung low
- Hunched or drooped shoulders
- Avoidant eye contact

- Disconnected from your physical body and sensations
- Constant visual scanning of the external environment, looking for possible threats

What do these different nervous system stress responses feel like in my body? Here are some common signs for me to recognize in different situations:

My nervous system fight response is activated when:

_____

_____

My nervous system flight response is activated when:

_____

_____

My nervous system freeze/shut-down response is activated when:

_____

_____

My nervous system fawn response is activated when:

_____

_____

Does my body have too much (hypervigilance, hyperarousal, or reactive) energy? Do I need to expend some physical energy (by cleaning, walking, exercising) to help calm my thoughts?

_____

_____

Does my body have too little (hypoarousal or low, shut-down) energy? Could my body benefit from some energetic activation (dancing, jumping, standing outside in the cold)?

_____

_____

Are my body's resources depleted? Does my body's energy need some rest and recharge (reading on the couch, napping, taking a warm bath)?

_____

_____

Do my conditioned muscles or posture send signals of fear or threat to my mind, keeping my fight, flight, or freeze/shut-down response activated, and my body unable to feel safe or rest? Do I need to shift my posture by standing up straighter and relaxing my shoulders to help send signals of safety to my body?

_____

_____

Meet Your Emotional Addiction

Cycles of nervous system activation drive our narratives, our behaviors, and our autonomic responses. As we discussed on page 58, after we experience a stressful event our nervous system can become stuck in a stress response, unable to return to a state of safety or balance.

At the same time, the body's chemical response to stress—which includes the release of certain neurotransmitters, or hormones—creates a felt experience of stress in our bodies. The spikes of stress hormones like cortisol and adrenaline can feel very intense. When our body is accustomed to experiencing a stress response, we may unconsciously begin to seek out situations or experiences that continue this internal biochemical rush. Those of us raised in homes with attachment trauma (*a lot of chaos, unpredictability, or unsafe childhood relationships*), often become stuck in our own emotional addiction cycle. Our mind subconsciously seeks and creates situations that align with our body's stress response. Without it, we feel bored, listless, unmotivated, or in need of *excitement* when nothing is happening. This is why so many of us are drawn to gossip, drama, unpredictable relationships, or entertainment full of adrenaline rushes. Even though these cycles don't feel good and provide us with a constant supply of stress, we are at least feeling something—for many of us, it's the only time we feel anything at all. At the same time, there is always so much shame that comes with this cycle because we aren't *responding* from a space of conscious awareness, we are reacting based on our past.

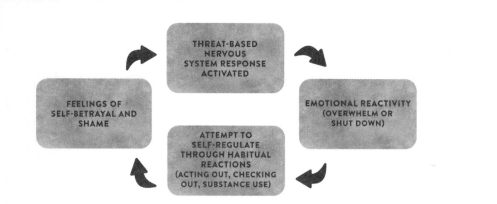

The Emotional Addiction Cycle

As you can see in the graphic above, the cycle of emotional addiction operates as a closed loop. First, our nervous system perceives a threat and reacts to it. Then we instinctively seek to soothe our reactivity in ways that don't serve us, leading to feelings of shame and self-betrayal. To break out of this cycle of craving and reacting (exploding or disconnecting) from emotional experiences, we have to do work on rewiring our nervous system. As you begin the following practices, you might find yourself feeling bored, or like you want to do something else, and that's okay. You might also have intense thoughts or sensations in your body. It's helpful to understand these sensations are always there; we are just used to distracting ourselves from them. With practice, your body will learn how to adapt to a life without constant stress stimuli.

Rewiring Your Nervous System

As you've learned, your nervous system responds to your internal and external environment every moment of the day, outside of your conscious awareness (through the processes of *interoception* and *neuroception*). Our stress response becomes activated when our current experiences are similar to past ones that were unsafe or emotionally overwhelming. These similar experiences are typically referred to as *triggers*, or cues of threat that activate our fight/flight or shut-down/fawn response.

Take a look at the various categories of triggers in the following list. Use the "Identify Your Triggers" chart on page 160 and spend some time over the next few days (or weeks) to witness and explore what types of experiences activate your nervous system's stress response. Once you have a better sense of what activates your nervous system, consider how you might be able to approach your triggers differently.

Time-Related Triggers

- Specific dates or anniversaries, holidays, times of day, seasons, days, or months

Environmental Triggers

- Specific places, types of places (*crowded or alone*), geographical locations, weather, or other environmental cues

Internal Triggers

- Specific sensations, emotions, or thoughts felt in your body

Sensory Triggers

- Specific smells, tastes, sights, sounds, and feelings

Relational or Interpersonal Triggers

- Perceived anger, disapproval, criticism, judgment or rejection, blame or wrongdoing, dishonesty or betrayal
- Feeling unseen, unheard, or misunderstood
- Perceived neediness (feeling directly or indirectly pulled to offer support or to rescue/fix/solve the problem/issue)
- Perceived pull for validation or approval
- Perceived withdrawal or abandonment, loneliness, or disconnection
- Perceived procrastination, laziness, incompetence, or messiness
- Difficult or overwhelming interpersonal emotions
- Feelings of helplessness or powerlessness over external circumstances

IDENTIFY YOUR TRIGGERS

	TRIGGERS *(time related, environmental, internal, sensory, relational)*	HABITUAL WAYS I TRY TO FIND SAFETY
SYMPATHETIC FIGHT-OR-FLIGHT RESPONSE *I feel unsafe and am attempting to fight or flee the threat.*	My co-worker criticized my work.	I make a sarcastic comment back to my co-worker.
PARASYMPATHETIC FREEZE OR DISSOCIATION RESPONSE *I feel unsafe and am shutting down.*	My co-worker criticized my work.	I check out and begin feeling disconnected from and numb to what's happening.
BLENDED SYMPATHETIC AND PARASYMPATHETIC FAWN RESPONSE *I feel unsafe and am trying to avoid the threat entirely.*	My co-worker criticized my work.	I apologize profusely for the mistake and beg to keep my job.
	TRIGGERS *(time related, environmental, internal, sensory, relational)*	HABITUAL WAYS I TRY TO FIND SAFETY
SYMPATHETIC FIGHT-OR-FLIGHT RESPONSE *I feel unsafe and am attempting to fight or flee the threat.*		
PARASYMPATHETIC FREEZE OR DISSOCIATION RESPONSE *I feel unsafe and am shutting down.*		
BLENDED SYMPATHETIC AND PARASYMPATHETIC FAWN RESPONSE *I feel unsafe and am trying to avoid the threat entirely.*		

Rewire Your Mind and Body for Safety

As we discussed on pages 58–59, our vagus nerve plays an important role in helping our body move between states of stress and calm. The good news is that we can influence the functioning of our vagus nerve to help our bodies calm down after a stressful or emotional moment. We do this by tuning in to or creating experiences (or aspects of certain experiences) that naturally prompt the vagus nerve to send cues of safety to the body. These are called *glimmers*, a concept coined by Dr. Stephen Porges.

Take a look at the following *glimmers* or *safety signals* and spend the next few days (or weeks) using the following questions to identify the different cues that help you access a feeling of comfort and safety:

- **NATURE SAFETY SIGNALS:** the sun, winds, sky, rain, earth, trees, plants, flowers, and animals.
- **ENVIRONMENT SAFETY SIGNALS:** homes/workplaces/buildings, the smells and sights of cooking, artistic decorations, the softness of fabric against your skin, the supportive design of furniture, the comfort of a modern mattress, a stack of books, and music.
- **RELATIONAL SAFETY SIGNALS: Self-regulation:** intentional deep and even breathing, calming or repetitive movements, and grounding your body in nature. **Co-regulation with others:** kind gaze, a smile/twinkle in the eye, a tilted head or other gesture of acknowledgment, receiving a response to our request, and cuddling with a pet.

What people, places, feelings, smells, and sensations help me access feelings of safety and connection?

_____

_____

What sensations or feelings do these cues activate in my body?

_____

_____

Now that you are beginning to identify what helps you feel safe, let's revisit the exercise to remind you of what you can do to regulate your nervous system when it's activated.

Widen Your Window of Tolerance

The term *emotional resilience* refers to our ability to cope with and adapt to stress. We can increase our window of tolerance by gently stressing our nervous system, then helping our body return to safety.

When we choose to do something uncomfortable, we give ourselves an opportunity to teach our body (*and mind*) how to tolerate stress. Building emotional resilience often harnesses the power of the breath or other actions we can take to calm an activated nervous system. In our mind, it is about harnessing the power of attention to redirect our focus away from uncomfortable and distracting thoughts.

On the following pages you'll find a list of suggestions for the kinds of small stressors that can help widen your window of tolerance. Make sure you feel completely safe in your environment before you engage with any of these practices. You can do these activities alone in your room or with a person or small group that you fully trust.

It's important to start gradually so you don't overwhelm your body too quickly. You might still notice sensations or thoughts that are very intense. As this happens, take deep breaths and send the intentional message to your body *I AM SAFE*. This will train your mind to have a different relationship to your nervous system activation, and you'll have more control over how you respond to future stressors.

	SAFETY SIGNALS (signs I'm safe)	WAYS TO STAY HERE BY MYSELF (self-regulate)	WAYS TO STAY HERE WITH OTHERS (co-regulate)
PARASYMPATHETIC RESPONSE *I feel safe and connected.*	I feel comforted by physical touch.	I can hug myself or cuddle my pet.	I can hug my friend.

	TRIGGERS *(time related, environmental, internal, sensory, relational)*	HABITUAL WAYS I TRIED TO KEEP MYSELF SAFE	WAYS TO REGULATE BY MYSELF	WAYS TO CO-REGULATE WITH OTHERS
SYMPATHETIC FIGHT-OR-FLIGHT RESPONSE *I feel unsafe and am attempting to fight or flee the threat.*	My co-worker criticized my work.	I make a sarcastic comment back to my co-worker.	I can take five deep belly breaths.	I can ask another colleague for support.
PARASYMPATHETIC FREEZE OR DISSOCIATION RESPONSE *I feel unsafe and am shutting down.*	My co-worker criticized my work.	I check out and begin feeling disconnected from and numb to what's happening.	I can take a brisk walk to the bathroom.	I can ask my partner or friend to dance to stimulating music with me.
BLENDED SYMPATHETIC AND PARASYMPATHETIC FAWN RESPONSE *I feel unsafe and am trying to avoid the threat entirely.*	My co-worker criticized my work.	I apologize profusely and beg to keep my job.	I can remove myself from the interaction and journal in the bathroom for a few minutes about what happened.	I can text a friend, asking them if they can talk for a few minutes.

BEFRIEND YOUR
Vagus!

Your vagus nerve plays a foundational role in developing emotional resilience by activating your nervous system's calming response after a stressful experience.

To help increase your body's ability to tolerate stress, you can practice consistently activating or *stimulating* your vagus nerve through the following exercises:

- Breathe more slowly (try for around six breaths per minute) and deeply, from the belly.
- Exhale for longer than you inhale.
- Gargle loudly with water or sing out loud.
- Laugh (yup, that's it!).

Cold Therapy

WHAT YOU'LL NEED: a large bowl, water, and ice

HOW TO DO IT: Fill the bowl with equal parts ice and water, then submerge both your hands in the bowl for ten seconds. Next, do it again for thirty seconds, sending messages of calm and relaxation to your body. Practice this daily for one week and notice how differently your body responds to cold.

Gentle Stretching

WHAT YOU'LL NEED: a mat or a blanket

HOW TO DO IT: Place your legs directly in front of you. Lift your arms overhead and then try to touch your toes. Bend over as much as you can without feeling pain or panic. This stretch is meant to be uncomfortable, but not past the edge of what you can tolerate consciously experiencing. Breathe for thirty seconds to a minute. Practice this daily and notice how your body responds differently to the stress.

Partner Sharing

WHAT YOU'LL NEED: a friend or a partner you feel fully comfortable with

HOW TO DO IT: Tell someone you trust that you want to share something about yourself and ask if they're in a space to listen. Next, tell them something you've been thinking, feeling, or dreaming about. You might feel awkward or uncomfortable (especially if you weren't seen or heard as a child) and may notice your voice getting tight or that you feel nervous, and that's okay! Just share. Afterward, take a few deep breaths and notice how you feel.

In order to begin making choices from your authentic Self, it's important to create some distance between the true *you* and older, reactive habits you've had for so long. Select a topic from section three (*ego, shadow, inner child*) that reflects the patterns you most want to change, and begin to cultivate one new habit that better honors your emotional needs.

Complete the following journal prompts (or create a similar one of your own) every day to help you keep your promise to form a new habit. As a reminder, each of us needs a different amount of time to turn an intention into a new habit.

Today I am calm and grounded in presence within the current moment.

I am grateful for another opportunity to practice being calm and grounded.

Change in this area allows me to feel more in control of my daily choices and responses.

Today I am practicing when I focus my attention on my breath to take a pause, helping to create space between me and my emotions for new, conscious choices.

Today I am _____.

I am grateful for _____.

Change in this area allows me to feel _____.

Today I am practicing when _____.

Congratulations on your progress! It takes courage to be willing to see so many different aspects of yourself. Now that you've done this work, you're ready to begin to meet your authentic Self.

AFTER PRACTICING THE EXERCISES IN SECTION THREE, YOU WILL BE ABLE TO

Understand and shift your core beliefs

Reparent your inner child

End cycles of emotional addiction

Begin the journey of rewiring your nervous system

MEET YOUR AUTHENTIC SELF

WHO YOU REALLY ARE

WHAT YOU'LL LEARN

What and who your authentic Self actually is

Why it's important to know your values

How boundaries can improve our relationships and our lives

Why self-compassion is key in a healthy relationship with yourself

Everyone is born with a connection to their authentic Self, the part of us that we call soul, spirit, consciousness, or essence. Our authentic Self is wise, accepting, compassionate, and loving. While we are all connected to our authentic Self at birth, we often become disconnected over time for the many different reasons we've explored together. Many of us were conditioned to behave in certain ways through what was rewarded (or *accepted*) and what was punished (or *rejected*) by our parent-figures.

When we consistently hear "You make my life so difficult" or "I wish you were more like your sister," we believe that something about us isn't worthy. We adapt by becoming a version of ourselves that is more likely to receive love or acceptance from those most important to our survival. Rather than listening to the intuitive voice of authentic Self about what is actually "right" for each of us, we learn to seek external validation. While it's natural to seek validation from others, when we do this at the expense of our needs, our desires, and our truth, we can become disconnected from ourselves and the world around us.

I spent many years disconnected from my Self, and woke up in my early thirties completely burned out, confused, and wondering why I couldn't just feel happy. I began to wonder whose life I was actually living, and started to think, *This can't be what life is supposed to be like.* The truth is, it wasn't. And I'm still on my own journey of meeting my authentic Self and learning *who I actually am.* This is exciting, and many of you might find yourself feeling eager to meet your authentic Self. While you might want to dive in at full speed, it's important to understand that uncovering your authentic Self is a journey. You can picture this process like peeling back the layers of an onion. Our conditioning (or *our inherited thoughts, beliefs, and behaviors*) all exists within. There's no way to "hack" or speed up this process, and you wouldn't want to. Revealing these layers is one of the most rewarding processes in life. Some people believe this is our true purpose: to discover *who we actually are.* To allow our life to be a beautiful living expression of our inner truth.

HOW YOUR AUTHENTIC SELF "FEELS"

Close your eyes and think about the last time you were fully immersed in what you were doing. You might have been engaged in an amazing conversation with a friend, drawing or creating something meaningful to you, learning about something you have a passion for, or just enjoying a day that felt relaxed and easy. This is called a *flow state*, and it's an experience we can only have when we are being our authentic Self. When we're in a state of flow, we completely lose track of time (we often call this *getting lost* in something) and our mind is fully present, relaxed, and engaged with the moment. We aren't distracted by thoughts of what we *should* be doing, or obsessing over what has happened in the past or what might happen in the future. We are just *being* ourselves rather than trying to force, push, or control what we are experiencing.

When we are in this state of *beingness*, we are open and experiencing reality as it is. Despite the reach of modern science and our access to vast amounts of information, there are still many realities or mysteries inherent in the human body, brain, and experience on earth that we simply cannot (and likely never will) fully understand.

These mystical or spiritual experiences that we can't put into words elicit a feeling of *awe*. Awe is a state experienced by our authentic Self that cannot be calculated, measured, or quantified. You've likely experienced awe when you've watched a jaw-dropping sunset, or when you've witnessed something that touched you so deeply that it stopped you in your tracks. Experiences of awe allow each of us to connect to nature's universal consciousness. So often our fears, beliefs, and conditioning block us from appreciating these aspects of life, as we remain lost in our own thoughts, feelings, and emotions. Our authentic Self is connected to everyone and everything and holds a deep appreciation for *all* aspects of life, for everything we've learned, and for the greater order that is always working with us in mind.

Now that you understand what the authentic Self feels like, it's time for you to connect to it.

Discover Who You Are:
Sitting, Silence, and Solitude

Your authentic Self is your unique, energetic fingerprint or signature that creates and animates all your life experience. Simply put, it is your natural way of being that guides you through your intuition. You may be able to call to mind experiences of being connected to your authentic Self; moments where you felt completely at peace, when you felt accepted or part of something bigger than yourself.

The *voice* of intuition is often not a voice at all and is instead a set of different sensations that occur more in the body than in the mind. For some, it is described as a pull on the back of the mind, a moment of inner knowing, a gut feeling, or a soft whisper of the heart. Most of us are unable to notice these signals because our attention is consumed by our thinking mind and we spend very little time discovering the various messages our body is sending. To truly hear your Self, you will need to create the time and space to listen.

While our intuition speaks to us throughout our day, it is helpful to practice attuning to its voice without the endless distractions of the external world. Outside of trauma and the lack of foundational safety in our bodies (as we discussed in sections one and two), many of us have been conditioned out of spending any time in silence or solitude to truly reconnect with our intuition.

The questions below can help you identify the past conditioning that may be preventing you from accessing your intuition. Recognizing these habits allows us to change them.

How often and under what circumstances (or when) do you find yourself feeling fearful or worried about sitting in stillness or relaxing? What are you feeling fearful or worried about?

_____

_____

_____

How often and under what circumstances (or when) do you find yourself feeling fearful or worried about losing control? What are you feeling fearful or worried about?

_____

_____

_____

How often and under what circumstances (or when) do you find yourself feeling fearful or worried about letting your guard down? What are you feeling fearful or worried about?

_____

_____

_____

How often was there stillness, silence, or free time in your household growing up? How was this time spent? How did it feel?

_____

_____

_____

What beliefs, if any, did you hear from parent-figures or other close relationships (school and peer included) about what stillness, silence, or free time means and how it should be spent? Did you hear messages that being still or quiet in your free time was "lazy"? Did you ever get into trouble for being still or silent or for how you spent your free time?

_____

_____

_____

Where is your attention usually when you are having a moment of stillness or silence? Are you fully present to the stillness and silence? Are you thinking or worrying about past or future experiences?

_____

_____

_____

What does *free time* mean to you now?

_____

_____

_____

How do you spend the free time you have available?

_____

_____

_____

How often and under what circumstances (or when) do you find yourself feeling worried or conflicted about how you spend your free time?

_____

_____

_____

CAN'T SIT *Still?*

Stillness and silence can be uncomfortable. Many of you may find it difficult to be still without becoming overwhelmed or shutting down. In order to become *safely still* in our body, both the vagus nerve's dorsal pathway, which contributes to your ability to stop activity (even thought), and ventral pathway, which adds safety to this stillness through an internalized sense of connection (or of being together while separated), must be activated. These two pathways, which you learned about on pages 58–61, work together to support moments of intimacy and all social behaviors that require stillness.

If you find it difficult to be in stillness or silence, it's likely that your nervous system is dysregulated, causing your body to continue feeling unsafe in these experiences. Keep practicing the nervous system regulation tools on pages 68–70 and 158–163 to widen your body's window of tolerance for safety.

EXPLORING YOUR RELATIONSHIP
WITH SILENCE

Now it's time to take a closer look at your relationship with stillness or silence. Remember, developing the ability to be silent and still will allow you to connect with your authentic Self. Spend the next few days (or weeks) beginning to witness the following:

How do you spend your time alone (or free time)?

_____

_____

_____

Do you notice yourself avoiding silence or always wanting distraction or background noise?

_____

_____

_____

When you are alone or in silence, where is your attention? Are you typically lost in thought or fully and silently present to your Self?

_____

_____

_____

When you are alone or in silence, how does your physical body feel? What sensations are present?

_____

_____

_____

As many of you are likely beginning to notice, you may not be spending much time with yourself in silence. Try to begin incorporating more moments of silent presence into your day. Even when you're washing the dishes or doing laundry, you can simply be quiet with yourself. If you find your mind is racing with thoughts, practice making the choice to return your attention back to whatever it is that you're doing in that moment. Use the skills you learned in the consciousness-building exercises on pages 26–33 to ground yourself fully in your own presence.

Find Your Heart Space

Learning how to consistently shift your attention from your thinking mind to your physical body helps you to reconnect with the voice of your authentic Self, or your intuition, that lives in your heart space. Your heart is the most powerful organ in your body, and it is constantly emitting energetic signals to the people and environment around you.

Your heart is also in constant communication with your brain, with each organ continuously influencing the other's functioning. Heart-brain coherence is now a widely studied pattern of unity and integration between the heart's rhythm and the brain's activity. This integration or coherence (or incoherence) has powerful effects on our mental and emotional health, attention, emotional stability, and resilience, as well as on our physical health; it affects our heart rate, immune system, sleep quality, and overall energy levels.

When your heart and brain are in coherence, you are able to connect to both your inner knowing and to the world around you. Because your heart often communicates with you through feelings of fear or constriction or safety or expansion, it will be helpful to begin to reconnect with this heart consciousness using the following practices.

Heart Conscious Practices

Heart Conscious Breathing

Elongating your exhalation activates your body's parasympathetic break, slowing your heart rate and helping to create needed safety in your body to reconnect to your heart space.

Heart Conscious Emotional Release

Regularly practice identifying and releasing any and all stored emotions like anxiety, sadness, and anger (see "Emotional Resilience" exercises in section three).

Take a moment to pause throughout your day to create or embody emotions such as love and compassion by calling to mind a cared for individual, object, or space/location while generating these warm feelings throughout your physical body. This quick act of embodiment will help increase balance in your nervous system, producing smooth, harmonious, coherent heart rhythms.

Heart Consciousness Visualization

This more expanded version of the practice above will give your body an opportunity to spend more time in the healing and connected state of increased heart coherence. To begin, find a safe and quiet place to spend a few moments consciously connecting with your heart.

Bring your attention to your breath, taking two or three deep breaths, elongating your exhalation and bringing your full attention to each deep breath.

Begin to focus your attention in the area of the heart. Imagine your breath is flowing in and out of your heart or chest area, breathing a little slower and deeper than usual.

Practice cultivating a feeling of appreciation, gratitude, or love for someone or something in your life (for example, your pet, mom, or comfy bed). Note: if this feels difficult or not currently possible, that's okay; continue imagining your life-giving breath flowing in and out of your chest area. Spend as much time with this exercise as you'd like and *practice as often as possible*.

TAP INTO THE INCREDIBLE WISDOM OF
Your Heart-Brain

The HeartMath Institute, a leading organization in the study of the heart-brain connection, has conducted experiments that offer significant evidence of the heart's wisdom. Researchers monitoring the physiological markers (heart rate, blood pressure, etc.) of study participants found that the participants' autonomic nervous systems responded in advance of being shown randomly selected pictures intended to elicit either a stressful or a calming response. These results revealed that the subjects' hearts and brains responded to information about the emotional dimension of the pictures roughly 4.8 seconds before the computer randomly selected them. This incredible research suggests that the heart is able to anticipate future events, and provides compelling evidence of it's quantum or energetic connection with the universe.

Practice the previous heart consciousness activities to reconnect with your heart, your most powerful messenger and source of intuition.

Be Who You Are: Express Yourself

You are the only *you* there is. Your appearance, your movements, your mannerisms, your actions, your thoughts, your choices are all extensions of your soul's expression and are all opportunities to be more fully expressed as your authentic Self.

Let's break down these aspects of our soul's expression into two categories:

How You Live in Your Physical Body

- Your hairstyle or headwear/headscarf
- Your bare face or use of makeup (ethnic adornments, cosmetics, glitter, gems, etc.)
- Your tattoos, piercings, or body art
- Your attire or the clothes you wear

How You Embody Your Life

- How you express your thoughts and feelings

  - Your way of using artistic expression to communicate your thoughts and feelings (e.g., journal entries, doodles, photography, poetry, painting, drawing, music, dance, etc.)

  - Your way of expressing your thoughts and feelings through speech (e.g., the words you choose to speak, your words' inflection and cadence, etc.)

- How you live and create in your world

  - Your way of cooking or creating your meals

  - Your way of arranging your spaces or environments (e.g., how you decorate your room; how you arrange and organize your furniture, cabinets, space, etc.)

The more you get to know your true, authentic Self (as you've been doing throughout this journey), the more able you are to make and embody choices that outwardly express and celebrate this magnificent, unique being that is *you*.

SELF-EXPRESSION CHALLENGE

hallenge yourself to bring your most authentic forms of expression to life. Spend a moment reflecting on the following prompts and write down your answers:

PHYSICAL BODY

What's something you've always wanted to do with your physical appearance?

_____

_____

_____

EMBODIED LIFE

What's something you've always wanted to do or try as a way to express your thoughts and feelings (such as painting, dancing, writing)?

_____

_____

_____

What's something you've always wanted to do or try that expresses how you live and create in your world (such as decorating or designing your dwelling/home)?

_____

_____

_____

Once you've identified some possible forms of expression for yourself, the work is to go out and *make them happen*! Note how it feels to begin aligning your outward expression with your inner authentic Self.

Discovering Your Authentic Flow and Soul Gifts

Flow states occur when we're aligned with our mind, body, and soul, fully immersed in whatever it is we are doing in the present moment. In our flow state, we don't stay stuck in endless thoughts and we don't overanalyze or attempt to change our internal or external world. Instead, we feel safe enough to immerse ourselves in the present, fully experiencing our being in that moment.

Your flow state will be unique to *you*. Sure, others may share flow states when immersed in similar activities, but your own individual flow state is born from your soul's inner self-expression. We each have authentic gifts, or soul gifts, that are natural and innate expressions of who we are. Some of us have the comedic talent of making others laugh, and some of us have the gift of natural patience to work with small children. Some have the gift of learning and communicating in other languages and some have the gift of physically moving emotion through dance. We all have many, many gifts, regardless of whether or not we are aware of them. The following exercise will help you discover your own innate soul gifts. Let's begin:

- Find a safe, quiet space where you feel comfortable and have as little distraction as possible.
- Ask yourself the following questions, one by one.
- Spend time in inquiry and self-reflection before you respond.
- Write your responses/discoveries to each question in the space provided, or copy both the questions and your responses into the notebook you've been using for this work.
- After spending time in inquiry and journaling your responses, spend the next few days (or weeks) to notice other present flow states.

When you were a child, what did you love to do?

_____

_____

_____

When you were a child, what were you good at?

_____

_____

_____

What do you currently love to do/enjoy doing?

_____

_____

_____

What do you feel good at?

_____

_____

_____

What feels easy to do?

_____

_____

_____

When do you feel most fully immersed in an experience or activity?

_____

_____

_____

Which experiences or activities allow you to feel that way?

_____

_____

_____

When do you feel most fully connected to the natural world around you? If you're doing an activity at the time, which activities are these?

_____

_____

_____

If you had no other obligations and a free day completely to yourself, how would you choose to spend it? What activities or experiences would you choose?

_____

_____

_____

Think back to a time when you felt the happiest or most fulfilled (this may be doing something you loved as a child). Describe how you felt that day. What activities were you doing? Who were you with? What environment were you in?

_____

_____

_____

Identifying which activities or circumstances allow you to enter your flow state can help you gain awareness of your authentic Self and what it's like to experience who you are at your core. As you become more familiar with your flow state, you can make conscious choices to spend more time doing these activities or creating the circumstances that allow you to become one with the present moment and world around you.

Notice and Celebrate Your Strengths and Talents

Have you ever noticed that, without our adult interference, kids are great at acknowledging and celebrating themselves? It happens instinctively for them. They'll say things like, "*I did it! I tied my shoes!*" or "*I'm so good at X*" when they've merely attempted something new. There's immediate awareness and acknowledgment of their effort, successes, strengths, and triumphs.

As adults, we tend to stop celebrating ourselves in this way. Most of us don't take the time to stop and notice or acknowledge ourselves (or we haven't been present enough to even notice our accomplishments). We rarely stop and take a moment to relish in our achievements—big, small, and everything in between.

When you notice your achievements and celebrate yourself, you're actually rewiring your brain to find *more* evidence of your strengths, gifts, capabilities and successes. By now you've learned that your brain has the ability to reorganize itself throughout life by creating new neural pathways that get stronger every time you use them. The stronger the pathway, the more it shapes what you believe to be true about what you can or cannot do. This is why noticing and celebrating your strengths and gifts is so important (and necessary) on the journey to healing and transformation.

After all, it's the thoughts, emotions, and behaviors of daily life that create who and how we are in the present. And who you are in the present—regardless of circumstance—is a magnificent, whole, complete, and divine being. You have come so far to be where you are today. You are *here*. And that in itself is something to celebrate.

Celebrate Yourself and Your Wins

Let's take a few moments right now to acknowledge yourself, and to honor who you are and how far you've come:

- Find a safe, quiet space where you feel comfortable and have as little distraction as possible.
- Spend time in inquiry and journal your discoveries to the prompts on the following page. It's suggested you copy this exercise into a notebook, so you can continue to revisit it and add to the list over time. Remember, you likely have many small triumphs throughout the day, like taking care of yourself (even brushing your teeth or drinking a glass of water counts!) or giving your time and attention to a loved one. Notice and celebrate all of these accomplishments!
- Keep this exercise active. Revisit your responses and add to them as you go through your days and weeks. Keep a running list of your triumphs, successes, and accomplishments throughout the day, much like you would write a grocery or to-do list.
- Befriend yourself and cheer yourself on for all that you do and all that you are.

Keep this in mind: your being here is a miracle itself. You've worked hard to be where you are today, and now the work ahead is to honor yourself. Let's begin:

What about yourself are you most proud of?

_____

_____

_____

What are your strengths? Name at least three. (Remember, no strength is too big or too small here.)

_____

_____

_____

What roles do you play in your life and what makes you valuable in them? Examples of roles include father, daughter, friend, partner, neighbor, classmate, and so on. Examples of what make you valuable include being a good listener, nurturing, helping to problem solve, and so on.

_____

_____

_____

What choices or achievements are you most proud of? Feel free to include things you are proud of today and any day of your life.

_____

_____

_____

What struggles have you overcome? Feel free to include struggles you have overcome both today and any day of your life.

_____

_____

_____

What are three things you have achieved/accomplished/completed this year?

_____

_____

_____

What are three things you are good at?

_____

_____

_____

How often do you spend time doing the things you are good at?

_____

_____

_____

How can you incorporate more things you're good at, or more of your strengths, into your day today?

_____

_____

_____

KEEP IN *Mind*

It's through the conscious repetition of new thoughts that we begin to build new neural pathways, so, actually *do* celebrate yourself for getting out of bed! When we *don't* create these moments to acknowledge and celebrate ourselves, we miss out on an abundance of opportunities to rewire our brain's old thoughts, beliefs, and patterns that often keep us feeling stuck and dull.

ALIGN WITH YOUR VALUES
AND PURPOSE

Values and purpose are beliefs that represent what matters most to us. They set the foundation for the choices we make and the actions we take, which determine how we exist in the world. Discovering and understanding your core values and purpose will allow you to create a life in alignment with who you are at your core—the highest and most authentic version of you—the version you are here to discover and become.

The more you continue to meet and discover yourself, as you have been doing throughout this journey, the more able you are to witness your beliefs and foster core values that align with your purpose. So, what are your core values and purpose? The following chart lists some values that might resonate with you. As you explore it, consider what ideas aren't included here that are important to you.

CORE VALUES INVENTORY

Accessibility	Challenge	Empathy	Inner harmony
Achievement	Citizenship	Equanimity	Innovation
Adaptability	Community	Fairness	Integrity
Adventure	Compassion	Faith	Justice
Altruism	Competency	Friendship	Kindness
Appreciation	Contribution	Fun	Legacy
Attentiveness	Courage	Generosity	Loyalty
Authenticity	Creativity	Growth	Self-reliance
Autonomy	Curiosity	Happiness	Spirituality
Balance	Dependability	Humility	Toughness
Beauty	Determination	Humor	Trustworthiness
Boldness	Diversity	Inclusivity	Wisdom

Explore Your Values and Purpose

In the following exercise you will be directed to explore the role of your values and purpose in your life. As you respond to the prompts, notice the first thoughts that come up. If you find yourself unsure of an answer, that's okay! Pay attention and notice even the slightest whisper of that authentic, intuitive voice within you—the one you've been uncovering (*and that's been guiding you*) on this journey.

- Find a safe, quiet space where you feel comfortable and have as little distraction as possible.
- Be curious, patient, and compassionate with yourself. As you ask yourself these questions and prompts, *allow space* for your responses to come forth.
- Write it all down. Use the space below or copy into your notebook. Remember: There are no right or wrong answers here, only objective inquiry, reflection, and radical honesty. This is how we allow our truest Self to emerge!

VALUES

What are the top ten values you most identify with? Another way to ask or think about this is: What ten values most strongly represent your sense of self?

_____
_____
_____

What in your life is most important to you?

_____
_____
_____

If you could be paid to do one thing that you care most about, what would it be?

_____
_____
_____

Who do you most admire? Why?

_____

_____

_____

What do you find yourself wishing you had time for? Why?

_____

_____

_____

What do you love doing? Why?

_____

_____

_____

What are some ways your current actions reflect your values? What are some ways they don't?

_____

_____

_____

What values show up most often in your professional life/at work?

_____

_____

_____

What values currently show up most often in life with your family?

_____

_____

_____

What values show up most often in relation with your friends? With strangers?

_____

_____

_____

Out of the top ten values you listed in the first question, which five most strongly align with your deepest sense of self? Another way to ask or think about this question: What five values are most essential to you and your future self? One by one, for each of the five core values you've identified and chosen, reflect on the following questions:

- Why is this important to you?
- How can and how do you uphold this value?

Write your responses and reflections in the space provided below.

VALUE:

Why is this important to you?

_____
_____
_____

How can and how do you uphold this value?

_____
_____
_____

VALUE:

Why is this important to you?

_____
_____
_____

How can and how do you uphold this value?

_____
_____
_____

VALUE:

Why is this important to you?

_____

_____

_____

How can and how do you uphold this value?

_____

_____

_____

VALUE:

Why is this important to you?

_____

_____

_____

How can and how do you uphold this value?

_____

_____

_____

VALUE:

Why is this important to you?

_____

_____

_____

How can and how do you uphold this value?

_____

_____

_____

What is your life's purpose? Note: *You* get to choose—no one else. There is no right or wrong answer here. Listen and allow space for your responses to come forth.

_____

_____

_____

What is your calling? What do you see yourself doing when you envision yourself at your fullest potential?

_____

_____

_____

How do you want to live your life? Remember: There are no right or wrong answers. Write down whatever comes up.

_____

_____

_____

What makes you happiest?

_____

_____

_____

When do you feel the most fulfilled?

_____

_____

_____

What moments have felt the most purposeful?

_____

_____

_____

What contributes to your overall well-being?

_____

_____

_____

How do you want to be remembered?

_____

_____

_____

What do you want to accomplish?

_____

_____

_____

LIVING YOUR
Values and Purpose

Identifying and understanding your values, purpose, and their subsequent importance is necessary in becoming who we want to be—*and* it is only the first step. In order to create true change and transformation, we must turn our reflections, discoveries, and understanding of our authentic Self into *action*.

We must be willing to take this awareness of ourselves and *make new choices that lead to new actions*.

We must be willing to give ourselves acceptance, patience, honesty, love, kindness, and curiosity in the process. That's the true work—to be the embodiment of non-judgment and self-compassion along the journey.

Affirmations

for Your Authentic Self

My reality is valid even if someone doesn't agree with it, or denies it.

What is important for me is different than what is important to someone else, and that's okay.

I am kind, loving, compassionate, and wise.

My intuition is always guiding me.

I trust myself and my own inner knowing.

I release myself from the pressure of never making a mistake and allow myself to grow and evolve from everything I experience.

I have gifts within me waiting to be expressed.

I am uniquely me, and I appreciate that about myself.

Every part of who I am is beautiful, and I love and accept who I am.

My truth matters and I speak it with grace and confidence.

The things that interest me deserve my time, energy, and awareness.

My purpose is unfolding every day.

I am on my own path, on my own time.

I am exactly where I need to be in the present moment.

CREATIVITY AND PLAY

As humans, we are *all* channels for creativity. Creativity is simply the act of harnessing the wisdom and experience of our authentic Self to create an idea or to *bring something into existence*. While it may not be in an area typically associated with creativity like the arts or music, we all possess the ability to create—to make something new and valuable or to engage with activities that are personally meaningful and fulfilling. It takes as much creativity to make music as it does to develop the technology with which to make or to play it.

Engaging with our innate creativity helps us to solve problems in a new way, to have innovative ideas, to improve our ability to focus, to decrease our stress (*producing an effect similar to that of meditation*), and even to encourage learning. Creativity allows us to interact and collaborate, whether it's finding a piece of information online or cultivating social relationships with other curious, like-minded people. Creativity helps us find solutions to our problems.

Growing up, many of us were conditioned or shamed out of expressing our creativity through our true thoughts, feelings, passions, and talents, or simply by being our Self. Far too many of us were urged or needed to ignore our creativity to focus on more "practical" matters. This conditioning often leads to a habit of Self-censorship, or withdrawing your true thoughts, feelings, beliefs, opinions, ideas, or any other aspect of your authentic Self-expression.

Signs you may be censoring your authentic Self:

- Feeling reluctant or timid to speak what is on your mind or share your ideas with others
- Avoiding/not having difficult conversations with family or friends for fear of conflict/how they'll react
- Feeling unable to share your thoughts with others engaged in a passionate debate; fearing rejection or attack, even if you have clear objections to what is being shared
- Holding back your thoughts or expression on social media for fear of social rejection or upsetting others
- Being in public, even in a car with another person, where everyone is singing or expressing themselves in some way, and your fear of criticism or ridicule keeps you from singing or speaking freely
- Agreeing with others to people-please versus speaking your truth

DO YOU CENSOR YOUR AUTHENTIC SELF?

Many of us grew up in environments where it wasn't safe to fully express ourselves. Unconsciously, we learned to Self-censor or hide parts of ourselves. This exercise will help you become aware of where and when you self-censor, to begin the process of authentic Self-expression.

How often and under what circumstances (or when) do you ignore or disregard your own feelings/emotions to appease others?

_____

_____

_____

Is there a situation/experience/relationship where you find yourself censoring your truth consistently? If so, which one(s)? What fears or worries are preventing you from your Self-expression?

_____

_____

_____

How often and under what circumstance (or when) do you stop yourself from speaking your truth because you are worried about offending someone? If you can recall a specific situation where this occurred, explore and note the specific experiences and what thoughts/ideas may have held you back.

_____

_____

_____

How often and under what circumstances (or when) have you stopped yourself from doing something you really wanted to do because you were worried what other people would think? What have you stopped yourself from doing? Explore and note any and all specifics if possible.

_____

_____

_____

How often and under what circumstance (or when) have you pretended to be someone you're not in order to gain acceptance and approval from others?

_____

_____

_____

Why do *you* think you don't speak your authentic truth or express yourself authentically? What do you tell yourself as a reason to do this? (For example, do you think, "I'm not good enough. My thoughts aren't good enough. People won't like me if I share"?)

_____

_____

_____

Unlock Your Creativity

Now that you understand Self-censorship and authentic Self-expression, you can begin to re-connect with your authentic Self. In order to open yourself up to the creativity that lives inside, you will need to open yourself up to *all* your uncensored thoughts, feelings, and instincts.

STEP 1. Be present to your Self as separate from your thoughts and pay attention to the current moment. Creativity (or *any new thoughts*) can only happen in the present moment. As is now likely becoming very clear, when you are not in this moment, you are usually stuck in the past, which results in reliving reactive thoughts, feelings, and behaviors. In order to be fully present, your body and nervous system must feel safe. You actually can't have a new thought or solve a problem in a new way when your body and mind are under stress. Continue to use the exercises on pages 68–74 and 75–76 to build nervous system awareness and foundational body consciousness.

STEP 2. To help you practice getting in touch with your true Self-expression, begin a consistent stream-of-consciousness writing practice. This activity simply entails writing down (*in a safe* *place or journal*) every thought you can be aware of without censoring yourself in any way. You can practice this exercise in two ways:

- Set a determined period of time to write (such as five minutes) or
- Set a determined number of pages to fill (such as one full page)

As you're practicing, witness how many times you try to censor your thoughts and begin to practice empowering yourself to write your truth, whatever it may be.

Play

As children, play is a constant. Everything is new and everything is an adventure. As we grow older, we are often conditioned and shamed out of play and encouraged to be "productive" instead. But even for those of us who may feel we have little time or energy for it as adults, play remains an integral way to access our authentic Self.

Like the children and animals you may care for, play benefits you, too. Across all ages, play has been shown to relieve stress, increase endorphins (or "feel-good" hormones), improve brain function (by stimulating the growth of new brain cells), boost creativity, increase energy, and even make us feel younger!

Play is done simply for pleasure and enjoyment. While many of us associate play with more structured and goal-directed activities (like board games or sports), it also includes any relaxed, free-spirited, or spontaneous moments or actions throughout your day. For example, jumping around on some rocks you notice on a hike, being silly with friends, or working on something new you find interesting. Play is more about the enjoyment of the activity than the outcome (winning or losing).

In my community, when I teach play, a lot of people are shocked that they can't or don't play at all. Some of them feel like there's a block that's not allowing them to experience it. This is completely normal if play hasn't been a part of your life. Everyone can learn to access it with practice and an open mind.

sing the prompts below, take the next few days (or weeks) to begin to witness your relationship to play:

What comes to mind when you think of play? How do you feel when you think about play or being playful?

_____
_____
_____

What does play look like for you?

_____
_____
_____

How often and under what circumstances (or when) do you play?

_____
_____
_____

If you can remember, what kind of play did you enjoy as a child? What were you doing?

_____
_____
_____

Do you enjoy being playful in the company of others, or do you prefer to be alone?

_____
_____
_____

PLAYFULNESS CHALLENGE

P ick one playful activity from the following list (or come up with your own ideas) and set the intention to create moments of play throughout your day. Jot down your intention or promise to yourself (maybe using your future self journal prompts!) and revisit daily as a reminder.

- **HOBBY PLAY.** Make time to engage with a new or old hobby by doing something you enjoy.
- **GAME PLAY.** Grab a board game or deck of cards you can play alone or with someone else. Turn anything into a game, like putting away the dishes with your non-dominant hand. Remember, enjoying the activity is more important than the outcome!
- **TOY OR GADGET PLAY.** Yes, adults can play with toys, too! Grab a set of Legos or Jenga blocks and build a castle, make yourself a pillow fort to spend some time in, or go outside to make and throw snowballs after a snowstorm.
- **NATURE PLAY.** Go out into nature by visiting your local park or playground and spending some time exploring.
- **ROUGH-AND-TUMBLE PLAY.** Get active in your play by climbing a tree, wrestling with a loved one (or pet!), kicking a ball around, or engaging in a game of tag.
- **IMAGINATION PLAY.** Tell someone (or yourself) a story; color, draw, or paint a picture; make a craft; or take an acting or improv class.
- **BODY PLAY.** Move your body through a short yoga class, go on a hike, swim in a pool, or ride your bike.

DO YOU FIND PLAY *Difficult?*

Even if you've committed to making the time to do so, some of you may find it challenging to engage in play. This difficulty could be an effect of an overactive nervous system response. When your body doesn't feel safe, play is the furthest thing on its mind, literally! No human can be playful when they are perceiving an active threat.

Continue to work on building safety in your body using the emotional resilience exercises on page 165. Small playful activities can also help safely stress your nervous system by strengthening the ability to move between activity or stress and calm. Begin to explore using some of the play suggestions offered and try out those that feel most approachable.

COMMUNITY AND RELATIONSHIPS:
INTERDEPENDENCE

Interdependence is a state of interconnectedness to others and the world around us. True interdependence allows all members of a group or system (from your relationship to your friends or partner[s] to your relationship with the global community you are a part of) to connect with one another while also being connected to themselves at the same time.

The relationship we have with ourselves impacts every other relationship we have. Most of us want to have deep, vulnerable, fulfilling relationships. In order to have them, we must be aware of our own needs and emotions. Without this awareness, we can find ourselves in patterns of codependency and people-pleasing that lead to resentment and disconnection from the people we love.

When we are in patterns of codependency, we know no difference between *us* and another person. In relationships where there is interdependence, we can fully express ourselves while also allowing another person to fully express themselves. Interdependence means our self-worth does not derive from the other person, and we can release the need to control their behaviors because we trust ourselves to navigate the relationship. In order to establish healthy relationships, we have to investigate our connection to ourselves.

Take a look at the following chart to identify the differences between codependency and interdependence.

CODEPENDENCY	INTERDEPENDENCE (AUTHENTIC RELATIONSHIPS)
Lack of boundaries	Intact, healthy boundaries (separation between self and other)
Chronic people-pleasing	Knowing your own values (what matters to you and for you)
Unhealthy communication dynamics	Feeling free and safe to fully Self express
Unconscious controlling behaviors	Not afraid to say "no"
Struggles with expressing emotions	Having hobbies, relationships, and interests of your own
Difficulty with emotional and/or sexual intimacy	Spending time alone and feeling secure in time apart
Blaming each other	Establishing mutual space for growth and evolution
Low self-worth	Asking for what you want or need
Push-pull behaviors (closeness and removal of love cycles)	Engaging in open, honest, vulnerable communication
No space for outside relationships, hobbies, or interests	

SELF-CONNECTION CHECKLIST

Since your connection to yourself impacts all of your other relationships, it will be helpful to witness your current level of Self-connection. Using the following checklist, spend the next few days (or weeks) exploring your connection to your Self.

____ I am able to set clear boundaries.

____ I'm able to do what brings me joy (from a place of pure intention) even if the other person doesn't like it.

____ I feel guilty or uncomfortable if I do something without my partner(s).

____ I am able to have a different perspective or viewpoint from my partner and feel okay about it.

____ I am (*for the most part*) able to take responsibility for my own emotional state.

____ I am able to talk about my feelings without fear of rejection or shame.

____ I can discern between my partner's *stuff* and my own *stuff* (for the most part).

____ I'm comfortable taking space for myself.

____ I'm able to hold space for my partner's emotions even when its uncomfortable.

____ I'm able to compromise and not focus on *winning* each argument.

Now, let's explore how our connection to ourselves plays a role within our relationships.

Authentic Connections and Relationships

There are two fundamental features that define authentic relationships:

ATTUNEMENT: the ability to hold space for and resonate with the emotional state of our loved ones. This happens in safe, responsive, supportive environments.

CO-REGULATION: the ability to adjust your own emotional state as you navigate stressful or emotional situations with your partner. This simply means you can both safely allow each other to experience intense emotional states and help support each other's recovery, or return to peace and calm. This also happens in safe, responsive, supportive environments.

Finding Safety with a Partner

As you've learned, we can only open ourselves up to connect with another when our nervous system is in the safety of a ventral vagal (or safe and social) state of activation. One way we can help ourselves and others return to this state of safety is through the healing power of human touch. We can use physical touch to self-soothe or calm ourselves when we feel stressed, anxious, or afraid. We can also learn ways to use physical touch with partners or friends. Human touch triggers our parasympathetic nervous system and it releases hormones like oxytocin, dopamine, or serotonin. We crave human touch because of these "feel-good" hormones and because it evokes a sense of security, love, and belonging.

It's important to point out that everyone has a different response and relationship with physical touch. Some people feel very comfortable with it, others might not feel comfortable at all, even with someone they *love*. Our body stores information about physical touch, and many of us have been touched in ways that didn't allow us to feel safe.

As you practice these exercises, keep this in mind and remember you can always take a break if you feel overwhelmed. If you practice the partner exercises, be sure to communicate with your partner beforehand and during so you both feel comfortable. The first exercise will be one you can do alone. The second will be one you can do with a partner (*if you choose*).

Soothing Self-Touch

Find a private place where no one will interrupt you. If you feel safe, you may choose to close your eyes. You can try each of these exercises, or you may be drawn to one specific soothing self-touch. Few of us consciously touch our body in a loving way, so this might feel strange at first. Try your best to relax into all of the present sensations, and within a few minutes you'll notice your parasympathetic nervous system being activated and you'll begin to calm.

Soothing Self-Touch Holds

- Place both hands over your heart and hold them there.
- Place your hands around your neck, feeling its warmth.

- Place both of your hands under your armpits in a self-hug.
- Rub your chest area from your heart and around your shoulders.
- Place your hands on both sides of your face and hold your checks.

You can spend two to three minutes in each of these holds while taking deep, slow breaths. You can begin to hold them longer as you get more comfortable.

As you engage with this exercise, remember:

- Say to yourself, "I am safe. I am loved."
- If intense thoughts or sensations come up, take a deep breath.
- On your exhale, release all the tension in your body.
- If your thoughts start to wander or you notice yourself wanting to stop, gently redirect your thoughts to the part of your body you're holding.

Partner Soothing Touch

- Find a space you both feel comfortable in.
- Ask your partner where they want to be touched (e.g., their heart, their belly, their hand, legs, face, etc.) and how (e.g., very lightly, lightly, or with a bit of pressure).
- Place your hand where they want to be touched and take deep, relaxed breaths together in silence for two to three minutes.
- After two to three minutes, switch positions.
- After you've completed one round, you can do another or you can pause to talk about what that felt like for each of you.

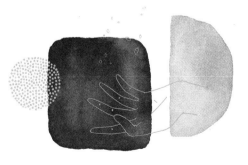

Relationships

Play can facilitate joy, empathy, compassion, intimacy, and can breathe new life into almost any relationship. Being playful can even help you regulate through stressful situations, such as new social experiences, by helping you connect with strangers and make new friends. Through play with others, you can safely learn about communication, boundaries, and cooperation.

If you find it difficult to be playful in your relationships, it's likely that your body is not feeling safe. When your nervous system is activated, play is virtually impossible. Continue to create safety in your body so that you can begin to integrate more playful moments into your relationships.

Self-Compassion Exercise

It can be pretty uncomfortable to notice the difference between the way we offer comfort to friends and sometimes even strangers in tough times, and the way we offer comfort (or don't) to ourselves. Some of us have been in the habit of shaming or criticizing ourselves for so long that we aren't even aware of this pattern. Learning self-compassion, or being a friend to ourselves, is the foundation of healing. We all deserve compassion, but most of us need to learn how to give it to ourselves.

We each experience difficulties every day. We feel stressed; we run late; we feel sad, unappreciated, or confused. This is part of being human, and we can learn to be compassionate and supportive to ourselves so that we can better navigate our life experience. *Think about it: when you're feeling anxious or stressed and you start to criticize yourself, do you ever feel better?* No. You just feel more stressed out and it becomes a cycle. The good news is we can unlearn these patterns and replace them with the self-compassion a wise parent would give us.

SELF-COMPASSION MENU

Take a look at the menu below and make a daily commitment to practice giving yourself compassion:

- I can take three deep breaths to help calm my nervous system.
- I can hold pressure points in my hands to calm my nervous system.
- I can grab my legs with alternating hands to help calm my nervous system.
- I can stop what I'm doing and go for a ten-minute walk to process my emotions.
- I can give myself a hug to support myself while I cry.
- I can write an encouraging letter to myself.
- I can stop expecting myself to be perfect.
- I can remind myself that I can get through hard things.
- I can remind myself how far I've come.
- I can call a friend who brightens my day.
- I can paint or write my feelings out.
- I can move my body to shake out its energy.
- I can put myself to bed early and remind myself tomorrow is a new day.
- I can remind myself I am worthy of love.
- I can remind myself I am safe and it's okay to feel afraid.

Now, take a few minutes to think back to a recent time when you felt scared, misunderstood, anxious, unworthy, or had any other overwhelming thoughts or sensations in your body. Using the menu above, pick a new way to show yourself compassion the next time you find yourself in a similar situation.

Think back to a recent time when you felt like you were going to *lose it*, or felt very out of control.

What did you do at that moment?

_____

_____

_____

What could you now choose from the self-compassion menu to do instead?

_____

_____

_____

Think back to a recent time when you felt really, really anxious about something that you had to do and couldn't shake the feeling.

What did you do at that moment?

_____

_____

_____

What could you now choose from the self-compassion menu to do instead?

_____

_____

_____

Think back to a recent time when you had a disagreement or conflict with a friend, co-worker, partner, or even a stranger.

What did you do at that moment?

_____

_____

_____

What could you now choose from the self-compassion menu to do instead?

_____

_____

_____

Think back to a recent time when you shared something with someone and you didn't get the response you wanted.

What did you do at that moment?

_____

_____

_____

What could you now choose from the self-compassion menu to do instead?

_____

_____

_____

Think back to a time when someone really hurt your feelings and didn't seem to acknowledge it.

What did you do at that moment?

_____

_____

_____

What could you now choose from the self-compassion menu to do instead?

_____

_____

_____

Doing this exercise, you will see how you typically react to yourself and begin to replace those habitual reactions with self-compassion. We can always choose a compassionate response, learning how to be a wise friend to ourselves rather than a critical parent.

THE INFINITE POWER OF *Prayer*

While many of us associate prayer with organized religion, it can be defined as any act of setting an intention or wish for ourselves or another. Research has shown that both thoughts and intentions can affect another at a distance, even in medically significant ways.

Begin to practice setting and sending your intentions to your future self or to another in moments throughout your day. To do so, find a few moments to sit quietly and to call to mind your future self or a loved one. When thinking about this future self or other, send them kind thoughts, compassion, and love.

**Connect with Your Heart
Guided Meditation**

Boundaries and Authentic Relationships

Boundaries are the foundation for every relationship you have, including your relationship with yourself. Boundaries are the limits we set around what feels safe and appropriate in our lives. Each person will have different boundaries, which is why it's important to clearly communicate your boundaries and listen as other people communicate theirs. By setting and holding boundaries, we teach people around us how to treat us.

In unhealthy and codependent relationships, there is typically a lack of boundaries. Partners might have no boundaries at all, or they might be consistently violated or ignored. All healthy relationships have boundaries. And emotionally healthy people are open to the boundaries of others because they know abiding by them will make the relationship safer, stronger and more secure.

Now that we have a better understanding of what boundaries are, let's consider the various types of boundaries we can create in our lives.

IDENTIFYING YOUR BOUNDARIES

There are three styles of boundaries: rigid, loose, and flexible. You can think of these terms as your boundary styles, and typically we tend to (mostly) identify with one style, though we can have different boundary styles in different relationships.

There are also three types of boundaries: physical, mental/emotional, and resource. The chart on the following page offers more detail about each type of boundary. But first, let's find your boundary style. Read through the list below and note the statements that resonate with you.

RIGID

____ I have few intimate or close relationships.

____ I have a chronic fear of rejection and tend to shut myself off from connection.

____ I have difficulty asking for help.

____ I am fiercely private.

LOOSE

____ I tend to be a chronic people-pleaser.

____ If people are upset with me, I struggle to function.

____ I feel extremely guilty or selfish if I say "no" to something I don't want to do.

____ I tend to overshare private aspects of my life with people.

____ In relationships, I have a pattern of being a *fixer*, *helper*, or *rescuer*.

FLEXIBLE

____ I am aware of my own values, opinions, and beliefs.

____ I feel confident communicating my needs or asking for help.

____ I feel comfortable assessing when and with whom I should share private aspects of my life.

____ I am able to say "no" and accept when others say "no" to me.

____ I am able to regulate my emotions and can allow others to express themselves even when I feel uncomfortable or if I disagree.

TYPES OF BOUNDARIES

PHYSICAL BOUNDARIES	• Your overall preference for the amount of physical contact that is most comfortable for you, as well as *when* you're open to or wanting that personal contact • Your overall comfort with verbal comments on your appearance, sexuality, or anything else related to your physical being • Your overall comfort with sharing your personal space with others
MENTAL/EMOTIONAL BOUNDARIES	• Your overall comfort with sharing your thoughts, opinions, beliefs, and worldviews without changing them to match another person's, or inciting someone to match yours • Your ability to choose which personal thoughts, opinions, and beliefs you share with others without feeling it necessary to overshare • Your ability to allow others to share as much as they are comfortable sharing; not insisting that others overshare
RESOURCE BOUNDARIES	• Your ability to choose where and how your time is spent, avoiding any tendency toward people-pleasing (while also allowing others to have that same choice) • Your ability to avoid taking personal responsibility for others' emotions, avoiding the tendency to play the role of *fixer* or to make others responsible for your emotions • Your ability to limit the amount of time spent listening to someone else vent about personal problems or issues

Setting Boundaries

If you've never had or set boundaries (*you're definitely not alone!*), the idea of creating them might bring up a lot of guilt. This is very common. Many of us have been taught that it's not okay to meet our own needs, have our own space, or protect our own energy. As you practice, you'll become more comfortable setting boundaries and you'll begin to wonder how you ever lived without them.

Some Reminders

- You want to set a boundary when you feel calm and grounded (*not during a time of conflict*).
- Avoid over-explaining. If we have patterns of people-pleasing, we might have a tendency to over-explain our boundaries or apologize for them. Practice stating the boundary and then accepting the person's response without trying to change it.
- We cannot control how people respond to our boundaries; what we can do is follow through with them even when we feel uncomfortable.
- Boundaries are kind. Giving people clear communication around how you want to be treated is an act of self-love. It's also an act of respect toward the other person because it shows them they are important enough for you to communicate your needs.

How to Set a Boundary

Sometimes, we can communicate boundaries in just a couple of words. These are called simple boundaries, and we might use them as we go about our day.

Simple Boundaries Sound Like

- "That's just not going to work for me."
- "I don't feel comfortable doing that."
- "I don't feel comfortable talking about this."
- "Thank you for the invite, it's not something I can do right now."
- "I'm not available."
- "I'll need some time to think about it; I'll get back to you."
- "Right now isn't a good time for me."
- "That sounds like a great opportunity, I just don't have space in my schedule."

Sometimes, boundaries involve more in-depth communication. These are detailed boundaries, and they include a follow-through behavior, meaning, *If x happens, I will do y*. Notice the focus is on I or Self. Boundaries are not meant to control other people. If someone violates or ignores our boundaries, it is our responsibility to hold the boundary, regardless of the other person's actions.

Here is a script for how to set a detailed boundary: The following script is meant to serve as a loose guide for how you can begin to set boundaries in your life. Adjust it in any way that feels most natural to you. The general script is:

"I am making some changes so that [insert your intention for your new boundary], and I hope you can understand that this is important to me. I imagine [insert your understanding of their behavior]. When [insert problematic behavior or experience], I often feel [insert your feelings], and I understand that is something you may not be aware of. In the future, [insert what you would or would not like to happen again]. If [insert original problematic behavior or experience] happen(s) again, I will [insert how you will respond differently to meet your own needs]."

Here are some examples:

SITUATION: Your mom continues to comment on your food choices and you've found this to be very upsetting.

BOUNDARY: "I am making some changes so that we can have a better relationship because I love you very much, and I hope you can understand that this is important to me. I imagine you aren't comfortable with my new way of eating. When there is conversation about my eating choices, I often feel uncomfortable eating around you, and I understand that is something you may not be aware of. In the future, I would like to avoid talking about eating altogether so that we can enjoy our time together. If comments about my eating choices happen again, I will remove myself from the conversation or experience."

SITUATION: Your friend continues to vent about her boyfriend and their issues, and you find yourself feeling exhausted and as though there isn't any space for you in the relationship.

BOUNDARY: "I am making some changes so that we can have a deeper connection and because I really care about our friendship, and I hope you can understand that this is important to me. I imagine you are going through a difficult time in your relationship. When conversations center around your relationship struggles, I often feel really helpless and like there isn't much room to talk about what's happening in my life, and I understand that is something you may not be aware of. In the future, I'd like to spend our time together talking about other things. If conversations continue to center around your relationship struggles, I will remove myself from the conversation or experience."

Now that you have some sample scripts, you can begin to build your own boundaries. Ironically, boundary violations are actually great guides because they'll show us what boundaries we need to set. On the following page, you will find examples of boundary violations and space to note examples in your own life. Take some time to consider how boundary violations may be impacting you, and what changes you want to make.

PHYSICAL BOUNDARY

VIOLATION	DESIRED CHANGE
EXAMPLE: *Your co-worker (uncle, mom, friend, etc.) consistently makes inappropriate jokes about your appearance and you feel uncomfortable.*	**EXAMPLE:** *You no longer want to be around these types of jokes.*

MENTAL/EMOTIONAL BOUNDARY

VIOLATION	DESIRED CHANGE
EXAMPLE: *Your family member (friend, partner) makes negative comments about your new food choices and you feel upset.*	**EXAMPLE:** *You no longer want to hear about, argue about, or defend your personal food choices.*

RESOURCE BOUNDARY

VIOLATION	DESIRED CHANGE
EXAMPLE: *Your friend (family member) consistently calls you at all hours to vent about their relationship issues.*	**EXAMPLE:** *You are no longer able to take calls at times when you are unable to take part in venting, especially in the middle of the night.*

Once you become aware of what boundaries you need, you can fill out this blank script and begin to practice:

I understand [insert your understanding of this behavior]. When you [insert problematic behavior] I often feel [insert your feelings], and I understand this might be something you're not aware of. In the future [insert what you would/would not like to happen again]. If [insert original problematic behavior] happens again, I will [insert how you will begin to respond differently to meet your own need]. I am making these changes so that [insert your intention for your new boundary], and I hope you can understand that this is important to me.

IS YOUR SPACE ENERGETICALLY ALIGNED?

Connecting to your authentic personal energy allows you to witness how you're experiencing the world around you, helping you to know if, and when, you may want to make changes. Some of us may not be aware of the impact of our energetic environments. You may be pushing yourself to enter environments that agitate, dampen, or activate your energy. By tuning in to how your energy responds to your various environments you may identify a need to reorganize your current space, or maybe to relocate entirely (whenever possible, of course).

Using the prompts below, spend the next few days (or weeks) to begin to observe how your space is affecting your mind and body.

Witness how you feel, energetically, in the physical space(s) you spend the most time in (like your home, office, etc.), including where you spend your down time. Note how this space looks (Is it full of objects or is there a lot of free space? Are your items organized or disorganized?) and begin to explore what aspects may be contributing to your energetic experience of this space:

_____

_____

_____

Witness and begin to explore how you feel, energetically, when you're out in your community or in your neighborhood:

_____

_____

_____

Witness and begin to explore how you feel, energetically, in your overall geographic location (with its weather, amount of sunlight, noises, crowdedness, etc.):

_____

_____

_____

Witness and begin to explore how you feel, energetically, in your various relationships (being sure to note any differences in how you feel around the individuals that make up each group):

With your immediate family

_____

_____

_____

With your various friends or acquaintances

_____

_____

_____

With your romantic partner(s)

_____

_____

_____

At school with your peers (*if applicable*)

_____

_____

_____

At work with various colleagues (*if applicable*)

_____

_____

_____

YOUR SOCIALLY COHERENT
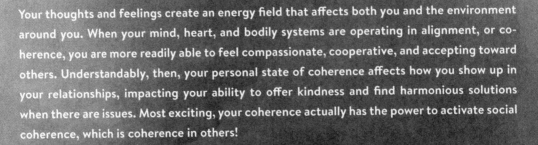
Self

Your thoughts and feelings create an energy field that affects both you and the environment around you. When your mind, heart, and bodily systems are operating in alignment, or coherence, you are more readily able to feel compassionate, cooperative, and accepting toward others. Understandably, then, your personal state of coherence affects how you show up in your relationships, impacting your ability to offer kindness and find harmonious solutions when there are issues. Most exciting, your coherence actually has the power to activate social coherence, which is coherence in others!

More research conducted by the HeartMath Institute shows that when multiple people within families, teams, groups, or communities activate heart qualities such as genuine care, compassion, and acceptance, the group itself becomes more socially coherent—or able to communicate efficiently, find harmonious solutions, and tap into collective intuition.

Using the exploratory questions on pages 218–219, begin to note the environments or relationships that promote a state of coherence, where you feel energetically peaceful and are able to access feelings of compassion and cooperation.

INTO THE UNKNOWN:
WHERE THE MAGIC HAPPENS

Many of us struggle to tolerate the idea of not knowing or understanding something about ourselves, others, or the world around us. Despite this discomfort, uncertainty is part of life. Instead of remaining fearful of what we don't know, we can learn to embrace the unknown and be receptive to life's mysteries. Finding curiosity, peace, inspiration, or comfort in the unknown allows us to remain connected with our authentic Self.

Using the prompts below, take a few days (or weeks) to witness how you react to mystery, uncertainty, the unknown, or the unknowable.

How do you witness yourself navigating new or unfamiliar experiences or challenges? Do you feel open, curious, and receptive or do you feel rigid, fearful, and reactive?

_____

_____

_____

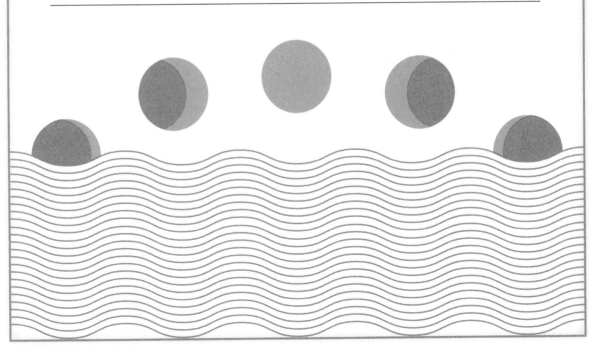

When you're not sure of something or cannot know an answer, how do you respond? What physical and emotional sensations do you experience?

_____

_____

_____

How open and adaptable are you to change? Are you flexible and open to it or do you find yourself panicking, shutting down, or feeling overwhelmed with fear?

_____

_____

_____

What pattern of behavior (such as scrolling through social media to research an "answer" or throwing yourself into work as a distraction) do you find yourself engaging in when needing to cope with situations of uncertainty?

_____

_____

_____

When you wonder about the mysteries of the world, what physical and emotional sensations do you experience? Do you feel expanded? Constricted? Fearful? At peace?

_____

_____

_____

EXPAND YOUR COMFORT ZONE

sing the list below (or making one of your own), set an intention to create one unfamiliar or new experience daily:

- Make a small change to your daily routine.

- Take a different route on your walk or drive to work.

- Sign up for a new class.

- Say hi to a stranger.

- Try a new food or cuisine.

- Join an online community.

- Sign up for a dating app.

- Try a new fitness class online or in person.

- Ask a partner or friend for help with something.

- Try a hike you've never been on in your area.

- Explore a new city or new town nearby (with no specific agenda).

- Start a journaling practice.

- Have a conversation that you've been wanting to have even though you're uncomfortable.

- Dance in your living room without any care about what you look like.

What new activities am I interested in or willing to try?

_____

_____

_____

Practice cultivating curiosity for these new experiences. Remember, curiosity is only possible when your body and mind feel safe.

CONNECTION TO SOMETHING GREATER

It is only when we are connected to our authentic Self that we can feel our deep and intrinsic connection with something greater than us—what some think of as nature, the universe, or a divine source. Communing with this larger force may take the form of practicing religion, honoring ancestors, experiencing the birth of your child, spending time outdoors, or getting lost in an art form that particularly moves you.

This experience of connection, or oneness, on a grand scale can be appreciated in small moments of awe. Awe results from an experience that both exceeds our expectations (or *is not like anything we've seen before*) and feels much more vast than ourselves (*like a sunset*). Our ancestors bonded over such experiences, coming together communally to witness the uncertainty of the unknown. Sharing moments of awe is a powerful way to connect with others.

We register awe in both our body and mind. Physically we may experience heart rate changes, chills or *goose bumps* on our skin, or even let out an audible gasp. Mentally and emotionally while our sense of self is diminished, we also gain an increased sense of connectedness with the world around us.

Using the questions below, take the next few days (or weeks) to witness your relationship to something greater:

How often and under what circumstances (or when) have you experienced the passage of time differently, like having a sense of time slowing down or stopping?

_____

_____

_____

How often and under what circumstances (or when) have you felt small or insignificant compared to the vastness of your experience?

_____

_____

_____

How often and under what circumstances (or when) do you truly witness and feel connected to the natural world around you?

_____

_____

_____

How often and under what circumstances (or when) do you feel truly connected to all other living things?

_____

_____

_____

How often and under what circumstances (or when) do you struggle to make sense of or comprehend your experience in its entirety?

_____

_____

_____

Become Curious and Find Awe

An easy way to cultivate curiosity and awe is simply to witness the world around you and focus your attention on what's actually happening externally rather than becoming lost in thought. Using the suggestions below, begin to practice more moments of curiosity and awe throughout your day:

ACTIVATE A CURIOUS MIND. While your mind becomes highly engaged when you're learning something new, both the novelty and your attention decrease over time. Begin to practice approaching even ordinary tasks with an open mind as if you were doing them for the first time. Lose any labels, expectations, or *shoulds*. Gaze at and fully notice even common objects (without naming them), presently and fully noticing their form, shape, texture, color, without any pre-judgment.

SLOW DOWN AND GET PRESENT. With known experiences, we tend to operate solely on autopilot. Deliberately slowing down your movements will help slow down your mind, so you can more fully focus on your current experience. Open your senses to take in what you're experiencing. *What do you see/hear/smell/feel/taste? What can you see that is new and that you haven't fully seen (or been present to) before?* Visit this practice regularly, and especially when you're feeling stressed or impatient with life.

EXPLORE THE QUESTIONS. When learning something, spend some time appreciating the journey of discovering new information as opposed to focusing solely on acquiring the desired answers.

BE AWED BY NATURE. Explore something new or vast in nature by visiting a nearby lake, park, animal sanctuary, mountain range, forest, or flower garden. Catch a sunrise or sunset or stand under the stars at night. Expand your awareness by noticing the empty space or edges of the life around you, like the spaces between trees or between you and the faraway stars. Visit these places regularly, especially when you're feeling isolated or self-consumed.

BE AWED BY CREATION. Celebrate the awe-inspiring artifacts of human creation by visiting a local library, historical site, house of worship, theater, concert hall, art gallery, or museum.

CREATE AN *AWE* PLAYLIST. Put together a set of photos, stories, videos, or songs that represent powerful, awe-inspiring experiences you (or others) have had. Visit this collection regularly, especially when you are feeling empty or disengaged, to help inspire a sense of connection to something greater.

Expand Your Awareness Guided Meditation

VISUALIZE YOUR FUTURE SELF

As we near the end of this journey, it will be helpful to revisit the same visualization exercise we did when we first began—imagining our future self! Now that you've spent some time getting to know your Self a bit better, you will likely be able to see clearer on what the future might look like for the person you are uncovering.

Remember to include as many details as you can when envisioning, while at the same time embodying the feeling of living this future self.

Find a comfortable and safe place to sit or lie for a few minutes and allow your body to settle into the present moment. If you feel safe to do so, you may choose to close your eyes to limit external distractions and help you focus on your internal world of sensations.

Envision your future, best, and most authentic Self, in as much detail as you can. Imagine what it's like to live their life. Imagine what they're doing, where they are, how they feel, who they're with. Use the prompts below to help you bring the details of this vision forth. As you call this vision to mind, continue to also embody the imagined *feeling* of being this person: *Will you feel a sense of freedom and expansion? Will you feel a sense of lightness and joy?*

Write down the details. You may choose to write your responses either here or in a notebook. There are no right or wrong responses here. We are simply imagining and taking note.

When envisioning your future self, consider the following questions:

How do you feel?

_____

_____

What are you doing?

_____

_____

What are you thinking?

_____

_____

Who are you spending time with?

_____

_____

Where are you living?

_____

_____

What are you most proud of?

_____

_____

What do you do for work or how do you financially support your life?

_____

_____

How do you feel in your relationships (with romantic partners, friends, business partners)?

_____

_____

What self-care routines do you have and how do you typically feel most days?

_____

_____

How do you typically spend your day (mornings, afternoons, evenings)?

_____

_____

Revisit this visualization as frequently as you can. Remember, consistency creates transformation.

Create Your Self

Now that you know how to connect with your authentic Self, you have the power to create the future of your choosing.

Complete the following journal prompts (or create a similar one of your own) every day to begin to make the intentional choices needed to take steps toward that future.

Today I am empowering my authentic Self expression.

I am grateful for another opportunity to practice empowering my authentic Self.

Change in this area allows me to feel more connected to my confident authentic Self.

Today I am practicing when I assertively share my ideas with others.

Today I am _____.

I am grateful for _____.

Change in this area allows me to feel _____.

Today I am practicing when _____.

AFTER PRACTICING THE EXERCISES IN SECTION FOUR, YOU WILL BE ABLE TO

Regularly celebrate yourself

Be compassionate with yourself

Place boundaries and create safety with a partner

Discover your soul gifts

HOW WELL DO YOU KNOW YOUR SELF?

Over the past weeks or months, you have likely gained an incredible amount of knowledge and self-awareness. To appreciate how far you've come, let's take a moment to revisit the quiz you took at the start of your journey.

I know what activities I like to do for fun or what brings me joy.

_____ I have no idea.

_____ Kind of.

_____ Absolutely.

I'm comfortable sitting in silence with myself and don't immediately need to distract myself or always be busy.

_____ I have no idea.

_____ Kind of.

_____ Absolutely.

I know what is important or meaningful to me in my own life.

_____ I have no idea.

_____ Kind of.

_____ Absolutely.

I know what inspires me or makes me feel uplifted.

_____ I have no idea.

_____ Kind of.

_____ Absolutely.

I'm aware of what my different needs are.

_____ I have no idea.

_____ Kind of.

_____ Absolutely.

I'm aware of how to ask someone to help me meet my needs (if I'm unable to meet them on my own).

_____ I have no idea.

_____ Kind of.

_____ Absolutely.

When I'm overwhelmed, I'm able to ask for support.

_____ I have no idea.

_____ Kind of.

_____ Absolutely.

I know when I don't feel safe in a situation.

_____ I have no idea.

_____ Kind of.

_____ Absolutely.

I know when I've reached a high level of stress or feel overwhelmed and shouldn't make any important decisions.

_____ I have no idea.

_____ Kind of.

_____ Absolutely.

I'm aware of what I am looking for in my relationships.

____ I have no idea.

____ Kind of.

____ Absolutely.

I'm aware of why I did things in my past, and I understand myself at that time.

____ I have no idea.

____ Kind of.

____ Absolutely.

I'm aware of when I'm not being kind to myself (self-shaming, criticizing, comparing).

____ I have no idea.

____ Kind of.

____ Absolutely.

I know when my body needs to move and when it needs to rest.

____ I have no idea.

____ Kind of.

____ Absolutely.

I know the difference between when I'm actually hungry and when I'm eating to distract myself or numb my emotions.

____ I have no idea.

____ Kind of.

____ Absolutely.

When I'm upset, I'm aware of the pattern of behavior I usually engage in (silent treatment shutdown, yelling, distracting myself/dissociation).

____ I have no idea.

____ Kind of.

____ Absolutely.

I know when I'm people-pleasing or doing something because someone wants me to, rather than because I actually want to do it.

____ I have no idea.

____ Kind of.

____ Absolutely.

FINAL THOUGHTS

Although this book may come to an end, your journey as a living, breathing human being does not, and it will continue to evolve as you venture into the future. Returning to these tools, especially when you feel stuck, stressed, sad, lonely, anxious, or unhappy with yourself or your world, can help you identify roadblocks in your path and restart your transformation.

As you've now hopefully learned, while they can be uncomfortable, transformation and growth don't need to be scary or overwhelming. By setting and keeping small daily promises to yourself, you can find and maintain internal grounding and rediscover your authentic Self as the Earth continues to spin, your body ages, your environment changes, and others in your life come and go.

Remember that this is a journey of discovery and rediscovery as we continue to grow, change, and evolve over time. Regardless of what happens, we have the power to create change each and every day and continuously unwrap the biggest gift inside us all: our authentic Self.

ACKNOWLEDGMENTS

First and foremost, I want to acknowledge every single one of you who picked up this workbook and who commit themselves to this transformational journey of self-exploration. When we heal ourselves, we heal the world. I am honored to walk alongside all of you as you create change in yourselves, your relationships, your communities, and ultimately our shared future.

To my partners, Jenna and Lolly, who are true co-creators of all of this work: to have found two others who share the same vision I am forever grateful. Your shared wisdom from your own life journeys helps me grow. Your insights, perspectives, and fearless ability to speak your own heart's truth challenge me to evolve my own awareness. Your love and support have created a foundation of safety for me to continue my journey toward embodying my true authentic Self. I love you both unconditionally and with my whole heart.

To my team, Brittany, Faiza, Furkan, Mike, and Tia, your dedication and support to the vision of this work allows me the time and space to create. Your embodiment of this work and individual evolutions continue to inspire daily.

To Dado, my agent-angel. My soul knows we were meant to connect, and I remain overwhelmingly grateful for your continued presence on this journey. You have seen, understood, and supported the vision from day one and remain a massive influence in every book I write.

I want to thank my publisher, Harper Wave, who continues to wholeheartedly support getting this work into print. Julie, your understanding of this work and editorial feedback helped develop and hone this workbook. To the rest of the team—Yelena, Emma, Amanda, and Karen—who helped bring this workbook into the world. Thank you to Leah, Suzy, and Jo who brought beauty and life to each page and exercise.

Nothing I create would be possible without my global community of SelfHealers who courageously do the work to change our world. I see, honor, and thank all of you!

FEELINGS WHEEL

E motions and feelings (or *our mind's interpretation of emotions*) begin as sensations in the body that contain important information about how we're experiencing our current environment. The Feelings Wheel can be used to help you identify and describe what you're experiencing.

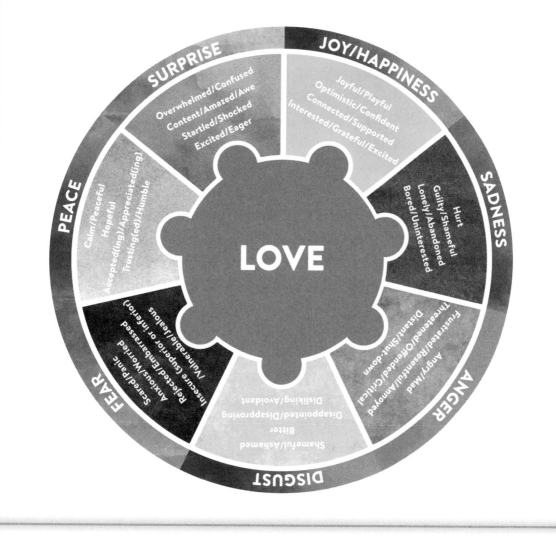

FUTURE SELF JOURNAL

Future Self Journaling (FSJ) is based on the power of neuroplasticity, or the brain's ability to change or create new neural pathways throughout life. FSJ is a daily practice aimed at helping you break free from your subconscious autopilot—or the daily conditioned habits that are keeping you stuck repeating your past. You can begin to move forward by consistently engaging in the following activities:

- Observing the current ways you remain stuck in your past conditioning
- Setting a conscious daily intention to change
- Setting small, actionable steps that support daily choices aligned with a new and different future
- Empowering and following through with these new daily choices despite the common and universal presence of mental resistance

The daily, actionable prompts provided throughout this workbook will help you keep one small promise to yourself each day in order to change a single aspect of what you think, feel, or do. This daily promise can be as simple as starting the day by drinking a full glass of water (instead of rushing straight for our phone, coffee, or the shower), taking the time to walk ten minutes alone without any distractions, or practicing deep breathing for five minutes before bed.

By practicing FSJ each day, you will be able to create new habits—new patterns of behavior—by overriding long-standing subconscious pathways, replacing them with new ones to help you be who you *want* to be.

On the following page is a blank template you can use each day to begin creating change. Feel free to write your initial answers in the space provided or re-write in your own dedicated notebook/journal of your choosing. It doesn't have to be leather-bound or fancy—it just needs to be a private space for your daily thoughts.

TODAY I AM present.

I AM GRATEFUL FOR another opportunity to practice being conscious.

CHANGE IN THIS AREA ALLOWS ME TO FEEL more connected with myself and others.

TODAY I AM PRACTICING WHEN I notice my attention has wandered and I bring it back to the present moment.

TODAY I AM _____.

I AM GRATEFUL FOR _____.

CHANGE IN THIS AREA ALLOWS ME TO FEEL _____.

TODAY I AM PRACTICING WHEN _____.

APPENDIX

ABOUT THE AUTHOR

Dr. Nicole LePera is a holistic psychologist, author of the #1 *New York Times* bestselling book *How to Do the Work*, and host of *SelfHealers Soundboard* podcast. She received training in clinical psychology at Cornell University and the New School of Social Research. Dr. LePera created the #selfhealers movement and gives free daily content to 6.5 million subscribers across social media platforms. She founded SelfHealers Circle, a self-guided global membership for community-based healing. She lives in Scottsdale, Arizona.